Don't ever Call me Ma'am!

The *Real* Cougar Woman Handbook
for Life Over 40

Don't ever Call Me Ma'am!

The *Real* Cougar Woman Handbook
for Life Over 40

Linda Franklin

MESSENGER
HOUSE
B O O K S
A PART OF ADVANTAGE MEDIA GROUP

Published by Messenger House, Charleston, South Carolina.
Member of Advantage Media Group.

MESSENGER HOUSE is a registered trademark and the Messenger House colophon is a trademark of Advantage Media Group, Inc.

Printed in the United States of America.

ISBN: 978-1-59932-161-5
LCCN: 2009908630

This publication is designed to provide accurate and authoritative information in regard to the subject matter covered. It is sold with the understanding that the publisher is not engaged in rendering legal, accounting, or other professional services. If legal advice or other expert assistance is required, the services of a competent professional person should be sought.

Most Advantage Media Group titles are available at special quantity discounts for bulk purchases for sales promotions, premiums, fundraising, and educational use. Special versions or book excerpts can also be created to fit specific needs.

For more information, please write: Special Markets, Advantage Media Group, P.O. Box 272, Charleston, SC 29402 or call 1.866.775.1696.

Visit us online at **advantagefamily**.com

DEDICATION

I want to thank all the fabulous females who

contributed to the writing of this book.

The women in the Real Cougar community

provide me with

my daily dose of inspiration.

I also want to thank my husband Roger, who

is there to cheer me on as I make my way

through this lifetime.

Hello,

I am delighted to welcome you into my Real Cougar community. This is your place for connecting with other smart, sexy independent women – all who are proud to be over 40.

Before you start reading this copy of "Don't Ever Call Me Ma'am" there is something I want you to know:

This is just the beginning of our journey together.

I know there have been many times I read a book yet still had questions...and nowhere to go for answers. As a member of the Real Cougar community, you now have a place to go with many different opportunities to continue the dialogue with me and many other women who understand.

And here's how to get started:

First, I invite you to visit my blog; an up-to-date, quick read where I offer valuable tips and information. And here's where to find it: www.therealcougarwoman.com.

Once you get to my blog, you can also sign-up to become a member of www.therealcougarwomanclub.com. This is my elite online membership community that is for women only.

It's a great place to let your hair down and bond with other Real Cougars.

Of course, once you are admitted into the club you can also join the special group just for readers of this book. This is where you will be able to ask questions and voice your opinions.

Here what some fans had to say about The Real Cougar Woman:

I am thrilled for you and all your success this year! I went back recently and watched your interview on the Today show with Meredith Viera. I was frustrated, because she seemed somewhat condescending, and really didn't seem to "get" that a Cougar Woman is anything but the character on Saturday Night Live. I believe that thanks to your work, these attitudes are changing!

Thanks for all you do,

Robyn,

Robyn Carey Allgeyer, Carey Communications

It's very refreshing to see a site that promotes the positive qualities of women who are 40 and over. I'm a little tired of seeing the media's exploitation of what a cougar stands for. Keep up what you're doing - I think it's great .

Thank you,

Kevin

And I am also offering you a10% discount on my new online teleworkshop - "My Next 40 Years" - Secrets For Mastering Life's Second Act. To learn more and to pre-register just go to www.dontevercallmemaam.com/discount.

Now, there is nothing left to do but sit back and enjoying reading "Don't Ever Call Me Ma'am".

Warmest regards,

Linda

FOREWORD

by asha bandele

Author, *Something Like Beautiful: One Single Mother's Story,*
former editor Essence Mgazine

Linda Franklin and I became friends three years ago, after she'd left her Wall Street life behind...and she is one of the most dynamic women I've ever met and could ever hope to meet.

In the years following her departure from the male dominated financial community, Linda did what appeared to be a complete shift in focus. She dedicated herself to finding ways in which women can tap into their feminine power and retain their youthful excitement for life.

Around this time, women over 40 were suddenly being portrayed, in both pop-culture and in shoddy news items, as "Cougars": Man-eating desperados, skulking bars and clubs looking to pounce on unsuspecting 20-somethings.

But nothing could have been further from the truth, and Linda was there to remind us of that.

We knew the Demis, the Michelle Pffeifers, the Diane Lanes, the Katie Courics of the world. We knew that those of us who were over 40 and in control of our lives, our beauty, our sexuality, our money, couldn't be less desperate about men.

So Linda made it her mission to snatch back the term "Cougar."

She began calling us "Real Cougars," and she set about putting a definition to the term that encapsulated who we really are, what we really feel, what we really need, how we really navigate the world, and how we really live.

And then faster than you can say "sexy," this woman, my friend, was everywhere!

From FOX AND FRIENDS to THE TODAY SHOW, there was Linda in all of her beauty, representing the truth of women across the nation who defied stereotypes, ignored limitations, pushed back barriers, and sang their songs.

Linda told me the day I met her that she looked at everything from beauty to fitness, from managing your money to managing your hormones and your love life. And it seemed in those first few months of knowing her—I was nearing 40 myself—for every question I asked, she had an answer.

"Aging is inevitable," she'd say with regularity. "How you age is always your choice."

I'd listen to that advice and her general sense that women were in a new place in the world, our status the natural progenitor of the feminist movement. We are running companies and countries and no longer do we have to be dependent on men for money or security. We are the thing itself!

That is, if we dare to take control of ourselves, our spirits. For that was Linda's loving admonihment: to listen to your own soul!

After all, Linda knew that as "Real Cougars" we are the ones being called on, asked out, flirted with by men younger than us and older than us because they wanted to be near what we had: confidence, strength, courage.

And Linda saw it, and she's the one who called it first.

In small circles and large ones, we'd complain about the vulgarity of the way we were being portrayed, the falseness of it. We'd roll our eyes, mutter amongst ourselves. Frankly, we'd bitch.

But beyond that, it was Linda who was the someone who saw that we needed a voice, a clear and resonant "Real Cougar" voice to validate what we knew was true about ourselves.

There are not enough words to express what I've learned from Linda, nor what I expect to learn as our friendship grows. But I can tell you that in this book are many of the life-changing lessons she's shared with me about health and love and beauty and wealth and gathering my dreams and my spirit and soaring. Open the pages and be renewed.

PROLOGUE

Every woman, whether she realizes it or not, has a Real Cougar just waiting to be unleashed. Living your life as a smart, sexy, independent woman is the best gift you can give yourself. So get over listening to what other people think you should do and start living the life you deserve. This is the time to let go of your preconceived notions about aging, about sexuality, about beauty, about relationships with money, and give yourself permission to explore all of your possibilities.

I know many women think that a "cougar" is a derogatory word used to describe women who only prefer younger men. Nothing could be further from the truth. A Real Cougar, a term I coined in 2007, is any woman over 40 who is turned on and excited about life. A Real Cougar stands alone and refuses to be defined by her choice in men. This fabulous female is changing the role of women today and will continue to do so for many years to come.

Achieving the rank of Real Cougar is a privilege, never an embarrassment. You have worked hard to earn your stripes, so be proud to revel in your accomplishments. For far too long, women over 40 have been pushed to the sidelines. You are mothers, business executives, entrepreneurs and teachers. You are a million things, but not the complete woman you have always wanted to be. Now is the time to change all that.

Take Beth, for example. She's 48 years old and after her divorce she made a conscious decision to become a financially independent woman. She never again wanted to rely on anyone else to take care of her and her 11-year old son. To help make that happen she decided to go back to school and get her MBA. You see Real Cougars figure out what they want and then take the necessary action to make it happen.

When I asked Beth if she has any regrets about her new Cougar status, she responded with an emphatic "Absolutely not." I was delighted with her answer because I know it's not easy to make the changes that temporarily turn your world upside down. We do it because we understand in order for a new door to open you have to close one behind you. Today Beth loves the woman she has become and here's why:

1. She feels good about being an attractive and sexually vibrant woman.

2. She knows it's never too late and you are never too old to live life to the fullest.

3. She realizes she can create the life she deserves.

4. She is doing whatever it takes to achieve financial independence

The one thing that best describes a Real Cougar is this: She has lived too much life to ever compromise the woman she wants to be. No matter what her age she will never pack up her wisdom, her spirit, her dreams, her beauty or her sexuality and toss them into the back of a closet.

Remember those fabulous females in the Dove ads? The idea of having women in their 40's, 50's and 60's reveal their naked bodies to the world, was a monumental breakthrough. When I first saw them on a billboard high above Times Square I just stood there and applauded. Dove took a big chance on their naughty Pro-Aging campaign and women around the world fell in love with it. Finally, there we were front and center starting to garner the respect and admiration we deserve.

So now it's time to decide what kind of woman you want to be. Are you the one who is willing to unleash your Real Cougar and take a big bite out of life? Are you ready to explore your marvelous potential or do you want to continue doing only what other people expect of you? At 85 will you regret all the opportunities you didn't explore or revel in the full, rich life you dared to live?

This book will help you break loose of what is no longer working and give you a blueprint for discovering what's next. It's my intention to help you make the next 40 even better than the first.

I am Linda Franklin and it's my privilege to be your guide on this fabulous journey into the phenomenal world of The Real Cougar Woman.

TABLE OF CONTENTS

INTRODUCTION

A Real Cougar Is No Sugar Mama

It seems these days that you can't pick up any magazine or turn to any channel without someone talking about Cougars. While I love that more examples of seasoned womanhood are being claimed in the public domain, I hate the vulgarity -- ***and frankly the lack of truth*** -- that accompanies how they are portrayed.

Last year there was a speed-dating contest in New York City that was billed as "Sugar Mamas and Boy Toys". To be part of this spectacle, the women had to be older than 35 and earn a salary of $500,000 – or have at least $4 million in liquid assets. There was just one rule for the men: They simply had to be good-looking. It didn't make any sense to me. Why would any successful woman want to be part of such a high-profile public-ity stunt? Think about it. Would Demi Moore, Susan Sarandon, Helen Mirren, Sheryl Crow, Katie Couric, Hillary Clinton or Oprah – all ***Real*** Cougars – allow themselves to be part of such a charade? I don't think so.

Let me ask you a question. Why is it that any time a woman breaks free from the conventional box society has placed her in, she inherits a degrading label? If she succeeds in climbing the corporate ladder, she's a "bitch". If she looks 10 years younger than other women her age, she's "on the prowl". And now, taking it one step further, if she is in a relationship with a younger man, she's suddenly a "sugar mama" or more commonly these days, a "Cougar."

While it may be true that more women over 40 are enjoying relationships with younger men, they aren't putting themselves on the auction block to do it. Don't believe for a minute that a Real Cougar is a lonely predator skulking in dark bars preying on younger men. She is definitely not the cartoon character that too many make her out to be. Undoubtedly, this negative image was concocted by the overly testosteroned fantasy world of our male population. Let's face it: Women are still the prime target for the good old boy's double standard. And the only way we're going to change that is to continue to excel doing it our way.

I am not denying that it's extremely flattering for an older woman to capture the attention and admiration of a younger man. But a Real Cougar knows their boyish good looks and washboard abs aren't enough to sustain a satisfying relationship. A Real Cougar wants a companion who is confident and has the emotional, spiritual and financial independence she possesses. *You will never find a Real Cougar flaunting her cleavage or her bank account to attract any man. She doesn't have to.* So once and for all, allow me to set the record straight: A Real Cougar is not out stalking young guys. It's the younger men who are standing in line to meet her!

The Real Cougar Women's Movement

In 1963, Betty Friedan published her ground-breaking book, The Feminine Mystique. It described the dissatisfaction felt by middle-class American housewives and how they were being pigeonholed by society. The book became a best-seller and galvanized the women's rights movement. *Today we are all part of a new movement for change. But this time around, Real Cougar Women don't have to carry banners or burn bras to get what we want.* We simply have to stretch the walls of what we expect of ourselves. *Decide what you want to do and do it.* And, don't let what other people say, do or think deter you from your right to be phenomenal. You must be the walking, talking example of a Real Cougar. When we all do that, one-by-one we will change the old-fashioned aging paradigm. We've come a long way baby, but we still have to break down society's outdated double standard. When that occurs it will finally be our turn to roar!

A woman in her 40s, 50s and 60s is not supposed to feel worn out, confused and unfulfilled. But nevertheless, too many still do. The push and pull of not only dealing with your own challenges, but also taking on the problems of your family and friends is taking its toll. Multi-tasking is throwing you into overwhelm and you're forgetting how important it is to feel good. *The ultimate goal for this book is to break through the boundaries you have imposed on yourself and open your mind and your heart to new possibilities.*

Feeling good is the doorway through which The Real Cougar Woman makes her grand entrance.

What Makes A Real Cougar Woman?

The Real Cougar is five-dimensional. She's been around long enough to have a range of experiences in every significant area of life. By now it's pretty clear what's important to her and where to focus her energy. So the Real Cougar is a woman who embodies these five components:

1. She knows how to keep her body healthy

2. She knows how to keep her beauty radiant

3. She knows how to keep her financial affairs in order

4. She knows how to keep her relationships nurtured

5. She knows how to keep her spirit fulfilled

Wonderful things begin to happen when you have all five of these components working for you. Think of them as a string of Christmas tree lights. To keep all of your bulbs burning brightly is a great accomplishment. If one or more bulbs grow dim it becomes increasingly difficult to send energy to all the others. It's worth the effort to make sure all of your bulbs are burning brightly. When they are you'll notice a big difference in the way you feel, the way you look, and how other people react to you. When I ask women what are the top benefits of being a Real Cougar,

Woman, here's what they say:

1. Being a woman who is authentically smart, confident, sexy and proud
2. Being a woman who knows what makes her happy
3. Being a woman who is proactive, not reactive
4. Being a woman who can handle anything that life throws her way

I love being a Real Cougar Woman. I love how the unique mindset of the Real Cougar makes me feel anything is possible. I love the way I can put my efforts into motion, then stand back and watch my dreams turn into my reality. I love knowing I'm able to handle whatever life has in store for me. I love that a Real Cougar is the PURR-FECT blend of masculine and feminine energy. I love that the *Real Cougar Woman is smart, confident, sexy and proud to be over 40.* I love that Real Cougars are raising the bar for all women of our generation and all the generations that will follow.

So how do you start assembling these necessary components for yourself? Before you are ready to go out and strut your stuff, you have to spend time examining exactly what makes you tick. *Why do you do the things you do?* Yeah, yeah, I know you've heard that before, but now you've got to get clear then buckle down and create what you want. Don't let another day go by without an open and honest evaluation of your life. It's the best barometer you have to measure the choices you've made up until now. If you don't like what you see, if happiness feels like it's just beyond your reach, then it's time to slow down and figure out what to do about it. It's time to get in touch with the woman you really are, not the woman other people want you to believe you are. Today is the day you are going to stop listening to that voice in your head that says you're not enough. I am here to tell you – you are more than enough and always have been.

If you don't appreciate the Real Cougar in you, how in the world do you expect anyone else to?

Wouldn't it be a shame not to indulge in all of the delights that seasoned womanhood has to offer? Of course it would.

Over the years, I have helped thousands of women gain a different perspective on life after 40. On my website, **www.therealcougarwoman.com**, and in my online community, **www.therealcougarwomanclub.com**, we offer help and support for the everyday challenges women face. I invite you to join us and start thinking of 40 as the starting point for finding out who you really are.

So, if you are a woman who:

> • *wants to live the life she has always imagined —*
>   *you've come to the right place.*
>
> • *who is tired of doing what's expected of her —*
>   *you've come to the right place.*
>
> • *who is ready to discover who she really is —*
>   *you've come to the right place.*
>
> • *who is ready for a nurturing, loving relationship*
>   *with the right man — you've come to the right*
>   *place.*

The ability to connect every part of your life into one powerful energy source is a wonderful gift. That is the gift you are about to give yourself now. Congratulations.

Chapter One

What In The World Am I Doing With My Life?

The process of becoming a Real Cougar is a journey – the journey of a lifetime. It has taken me years to develop my special gifts and I am still learning new and valuable lessons almost every day. Today I am a woman two decades past her 40th birthday, and there is one thing I now know for sure: Each New Year brings with it a truckload of challenges. Even now there are times when life takes me into an entirely new direction. The only difference is that now I have learned to trust I will be okay wherever I end up.

In order for you to understand why being a Real Cougar is so important to me, I have to take you back and fill in some personal background. I hope that my story will help illustrate how all things are possible, and that you really do control your own destiny.

I was born and raised in Toronto, Canada, the only child of parents who were married for 71 years. Mom was 98 ½ when she passed away and Dad was 95. (Guess Mom was a cougar before her time!) It took them 15 years to produce me because of complications from previous unsuccessful pregnancies. They told everyone that I was worth the long wait, but somehow it was hard for them to convey that same message to me. I don't ever remember feeling special or being treated like the long awaited golden child. My childhood wasn't filled with fun times and lots of friends. It was filled with loneliness, struggles and disappointments. Mom and Dad led a pretty isolated life which meant I never learned the art of making or maintaining friendships. They were also products of the depression so in our family money was meant to be saved not used to enjoy life. We weren't poor, but extremely frugal. As a result, I wasn't exposed to or nurtured in the wealth of beauty and excitement the world had to offer. It was more about struggle.

During high school I shot low and made it. I always had a fire in my belly but wasn't sure what to do with it. I believed I wasn't smart enough to go to college so I never even tried. I became the victim of my own limited vision. I chose safe rather than risk the pain of failing. After graduation I honed my secretarial skills and went to work in an office.

When it was time for my vacation, my girlfriend and I chose to spend a week at a resort in the Pocono Mountains of Pennsylvania. (For all you younger Cougars it was the 1960's version of Club Med!) It was there that I met the man I am still sharing my life with today. His name is Roger.

When our week was over, my friend and I decided to go to New York to do a little shopping. Roger provided our ride. Before leaving he handed me his business card on which he had written where and when to meet him. At the prescribed time we piled into his aqua blue Pontiac Catalina convertible and two hours later he dropped us off in front of our hotel. I thought I might hear from him after that, but it didn't happen. I wasn't too disappointed. I thought he was a great guy but he didn't make my heart skip a beat.

I had been home for about a week when something happened that would change my life forever. While going through my purse I came across Roger's business card. That's how the fickle finger of fate came into play -- If he hadn't given me his card, or if I had thrown it away, I would never have known how to contact him. But here it was right in the palm of my hand. I decided to send a card thanking him for being so nice. He wrote back and that's how our relationship began.

Roger visited me in Toronto 2 or 3 times, and then invited me to spend the weekend with him in New York. By this time my heart was skipping lots of beats and I was really falling for him. Do you remember the song by Manhattan Transfer, "Boy from New York City"? Well, cool kitties, he represented everything exciting and glamorous to me. This guy swept me off my feet. He was the first man to ever pay attention to me. My mind was racing with fantasies of a diamond ring and our glamorous life together in the Big Apple. Well, can you blame me? On Saturday night I met a group of his friends for dinner. We ate at a charming little French bistro on East 31st Street. There were 3 other couples, all in their mid 20's, all married, all college graduates, all with a sparkle in their eye and their lives on the runway ready for takeoff. I remember thinking, "I wish I was them." They had what I wanted. Sitting through that dinner was torture for me. As the night wore on a deep wave of emotion swept over me and it almost knocked me off my chair. I felt dumb, inadequate, sad and very much out-of-place. I barely said a word during dinner because I was afraid any-thing I would say would sound stupid. Here I was again, telling myself I couldn't measure up. When we got back to the hotel, I started to sob. Then came the first of many times throughout my life when I found myself asking, ***"What in the world am I doing with my life?"***

That night I told Roger things I had never said out loud before. The floodgates opened and the truth came pouring out. I said, "I am absolutely miserable! I am still living at home! I have a job that I hate! I don't feel loved! I don't have a dream! I don't have a college degree! And what's worse, I have no idea of how to make things better." He listened and the only thing he said was, "You are a diamond in the rough with so much possibil-ity." Of course, I didn't believe that for a minute.

After a rocky year of an on and off relationship I did something crazy, probably the first really impulsive thing I had ever done in my life. I packed my bags and announced to my parents that I was moving to New York. When I told Roger he was flabber-gasted because we had never even discussed it, and he certainly hadn't invited me to come. I just decided to make a change and hope for the best.

When I arrived I found a small furnished apartment facing a brick wall and got another secretarial job. Our relationship continued being an on and off thing – him running away when he felt things were moving too fast. So nothing much had changed, except for the geography. I was still confused and very far away from figuring out how to create my own happiness. Back then my joy was totally dependent on other people's behavior. That's a pretty painful way to go through life, wouldn't you agree?

Finally, on the eve of my 29th birthday, my life began to change for the better. Just like finding Roger's business card, this was another one of those defining moments that hit you when you least expect it.

It was a Friday night and on the way home from work I stopped and bought myself a couple of self-help books I don't remember what prompted me to go into the book store that night, but that really doesn't matter. Anyway I got home, crawled into bed and started to read. Then something crazy started to happen. I began to feel a series of electric shocks running through my body. Nothing like that had ever happened before but for some reason I wasn't scared. It actually felt good - like a switch was turned on and now I could see what had been missing all my life. As I kept reading I literally felt like I was on fire. For the first time ever, I knew I had the power to change things. I knew I didn't have to wait for anyone else to make me happy. I knew my happiness was an inside job. I knew I had the ability to create the circumstances that would change my life. I believe that night was the beginning of my transformation into the woman I had always hoped I could be.

Over the next months I asked for opportunities I would have been too afraid to ask for in the past. For three years I had been working as a secretary for a Wall Street investment firm, but I knew I wanted more. One Monday morning I walked into my boss's office and asked for the chance to work in the firm's trading department. He looked up at me over the top of his glasses and said "Okay Linda. If that's what you want, you can give it a try, but if you don't make it, you're fired." It was at that moment I knew it was "damn the torpedoes – full speed ahead!"

The next twenty years were truly amazing. My newfound beliefs kept propelling me forward. I was creating the career of a lifetime. I became the first Canadian woman to own a seat on The New York Stock Exchange. I ran my firm's arbitrage trading department. I was the first female to ever make partner in this totally male bastion. I was kicking ass. For the first time in my life I felt like I had what it takes to be a total success.

I had learned a lot about being a Real Cougar over those two decades, but I was about to find out that I didn't know nearly enough.

Do you know what to do if you want to make God laugh? Make plans! I found out for myself how true that is. Since change is a constant we are always going to be presented with new challenges. I had planned to stay on Wall Street until they carried me out feet first, but that's not what happened. I found myself caught up in a series of circumstances that started to once again shake my faith in myself. The foundation I had built over the past 20 years was beginning to crumble and crumble fast.

Do you know what to do if you want to make God laugh? Make plans!

At 49 I was swallowed up by what I now call the "Tsunami of Change". My body was changing, my beauty was fading, my spirit was unraveling, and I started to feel the intense pressure of the job. My thoughts were now focused away from my abilities and onto the young turks who were angling for my position. For the first time in a long time fear had taken over and I started to cascade into a downward spiral. I no longer felt I was capable of managing the hundreds of millions of dollars I was in charge of trading, so I stepped down. I walked away from the career that I felt defined me. The day I closed the door to my office for the last time was the toughest day of my entire life. I shall never forget it.

At 49 I was swallowed up by what I now call the "Tsunami of Change".

That first morning without my work was devastating. I was completely lost. I didn't know whether to stay in bed or get up and get dressed. At the office I made hundreds of major decisions everyday. Now, all of a sudden what to do with my day seemed monumental. When I finally made it from the bedroom to the bathroom, I looked into the mirror and screamed: ***"What in the world am I doing with my life?"*** I didn't have an answer. I felt as lost and desolate as the first time I asked myself that same question at 19. All of the woulda, shoulda, coulda's, were running wild in my mind.

Things got progressively worse. I was trapped in my own nightmare. People kept asking me how it felt to be retired and that was excruciating. Every time someone asked what I was going to do now it felt like a dagger in my heart. I had no idea what to do or what to say so it was easier just to disappear. I dug myself a hole and crawled inside. My hole had only 4 things in it – my bed – my pajamas – my TV and the refrigerator. This is where I lived for the next year. I was so lost, so angry, and so sad that I truly believed I would never feel the joy of being happy ever again.

Then, one day while watching Oprah (who had become my new best friend) I decided to end my own personal pity party. I remember it was one of her "inspirational women" shows, but I wasn't feeling inspired. In fact, all I did feel was jealous. I was jealous of the women who were doing something productive with their lives while I was just letting mine pass by. Before the show ended I made a conscious decision to crawl out of my hole and take back my power. For the last year it had been easier to hide but that afternoon I asked myself the question ***"What in the world am I doing with my life?"*** and the answer came back loud and clear. Find out why this happened to me. I had a numerous questions that needed answers. Over the last year I had beat myself up a million times wondering how I could have become so scared and insecure about who I was. Now it was time to get off my butt and find out. And that's what I did. I remember thinking, "Here I go again". Changing direction all over again - first at 19, then 29, and now at 49. It didn't seem to matter how old I was, I was compelled to keep moving forward. The first thing on my agenda was to find out everything I could about menopause. I was tired of hot flashes, sleepless nights, low sexual desire, and feeling blue. To get the answers I interviewed many doctors -- so many as a matter of fact that it was hard to keep track. Eventually, through my research, I found the cutting edge physicians that made such a difference in the way I felt. With my new hormone regime, the brain fog was lifting and the passion was once again starting to burn through.

I then spent months at a friend's aesthetic medicine clinic learning about the procedures that erased time from your face without surgery. What I learned there was truly amazing. Did you know you could take 10 years off your face in just 40 minutes? Watching the attitudes of people change as the sags, bags and wrinkles disappeared showed me how important it is to feel good about the way you look. Your self-image affects so many segments of your life.

I attended spiritual retreats, being mentored in person by the very people whose books had helped me over the years. Slowly I was beginning to reconnect with the amazing power of the human spirit. Now with all the new practices I was being taught, I realized what I had learned at 29 was just the tip of the iceberg. Now I was tapping into a much larger and deeper reservoir. I was learning to appreciate me for who I was, and not for how hard I could work. That was a huge step.

The year passed and I when I looked back I was amazed to see how far I had come. I had gathered so much valuable informa-

I was learning to appreciate me for who I was, and not for how hard I could work.

tion during my journey. I felt enriched in body, mind and spirit. Now, it was time for me to share what I had learned with other women who were experiencing their own "Tsunami of Change".

Starting The Real Cougar Woman has opened a whole new world for me. It's a labor of love that pays unbelievable dividends. It's a big part of an overall spiritual healing. To be able to connect with so many wonderful women is a dream come true. Today the business is growing by leaps and bounds and in addition to the blog there is an online support community for Real Cougars, a weekly radio show, rejuvenation makeovers, retreats, online tele-workshops, and a pro-aging boutique. My work has shown me that you can re-invent yourself at any age. I have helped thousands of women change direction and today they see life after 40 very differently. It's not an end after all-- it's a beginning of something brand new and wonderful.

So how do you find the strength and the resolve to gain this kind of perspective? How do you begin the search for the Real Cougar Woman inside of you?" Ask yourself ***"What in the world am I doing with my life?"*** Then take a deep breath, relax and listen closely for the answer.

Chapter Two

Your Tsunami
Of Change

Go put on your sneakers. It's time to hit the ground running. And, while you are tying your shoelaces keep reminding yourself that change doesn't begin with baby steps like you've been told in the past. Once you are serious about tackling change you need to build up a head of steam and then keep that momentum moving. The truth is, if you don't see change happening quickly you will stop trying.

It's important that you learn to think out of the box, and you've come to the right place to do that. Real Cougars are constantly knocking down walls or busting through glass ceilings wherever they go. Look at Hillary Clinton. She was a hair's breath away from becoming our next president. Hillary always has a big dream and does whatever it takes to make it come true. So what are your dreams? What are you willing to do to see them come true? Yes, it begins and ends with you.

If you don't see change happening quickly you will stop trying.

Am I ready to embrace change even when I'm not sure where it's going to take me?

I have thought a lot about this complex process called change and this is the conclusion I have come to: There are changes we consciously decide to make like losing weight, or getting a divorce. Then there are those unpredictable changes that come at us when we least expect them. In both cases the successful outcome rests in your hands. This is the question you always need to ask yourself: Am I ready to embrace change even when I'm not sure where it's going to take me? Think about your answer carefully because ultimately it will shape your destiny.

Lisa's Story

Lisa Lockwood is a member of my Real Cougar Woman Club and we talk quite often. Lisa is no stranger to change. From humble beginnings as a victim of domestic violence, she reinvented herself to become a Miss Illinois-USA contestant in 1988, a U.S. Air Force Desert Storm veteran, the first (and only) female member of her S.W.A.T team, and a highly decorated narcotics and undercover detective in Chicago. She is a woman who took charge and changed her destiny.

Her story is really a tough one to tell, but it's a wonderful testament to the resilience of the human spirit. Unfortunately, too many women have found themselves in situations similar to Lisa's and that's why I wanted to include it in this book.

Lisa grew up living in an abusive household which of course left very deep scars on her psyche. As a young woman she continued the cycle of abuse by choosing a man much like her father. Although she knew her fiancé had a terrible temper and a drinking problem she married him anyway. Why? Because she was afraid of being alone, afraid of change and didn't know any better. When you don't see a better way even abuse can become your normal.

Lisa's marriage was horrific right from the beginning. She endured more than anybody should ever have to. Lisa never asked for help because she was so ashamed of living her life as a victim. It was important to her that others believed she was a strong, independent woman so she kept her nightmare a secret. This cycle of shame lasted for years. (Shame keeps so many women tethered to what is.)

Then one night something happened. Tony stepped over the line. I won't go into what he did but it became the straw that broke the camel's back. Lisa was done and that night made a conscious decision to leave. She began to create her escape strategy. Part of that strategy involved becoming a police officer because she knew that the uniform would give her the courage she needed to break away once and for all. (It's important that you do whatever you need to do to increase your odds of a successful transition).

Lisa put her plan into action and it worked. She not only succeeded in divorcing Tony, but she managed to work herself up through the ranks of the Chicago Police Department. From there she went on to become the first female member of their elite S.W.A.T Team. After receiving the prestigious title of "Officer of the Year", Lisa knew it was time to change her life yet again. This time it would be to pursue her true passion, a dream she had carried with her for a very long time. She wanted to teach women how to achieve success, not only in their personal lives, but triumph in male-dominated careers despite daunting obstacles from their past.

Today Lisa is 40 and married to the man of her dreams. She is a step-mom to three children and is pursuing a speaking and coaching career. Her book Undercover Angel: From Beauty Queen to S. W. A. T. *Team helped her to heal and now she has been approached by Hollywood who want to tell her story. You can find out more about Lisa at www.lisalockwood.com.*

Gracefully Moving Through Change

Lisa is a great example of how it takes more than a dream to create change. It takes a shift in our behavior. It takes choosing to go after the "what's possible" rather than holding on to the "what is". Always opting for the "what is" because we believe it's easier ultimately makes us a victim. Over time our fears can turn us into a person we don't even recognize. For too many fear has turned us into control freaks.

You might be wondering what is the connection between fear and control? Here's what I believe and I talk from personal experience. When you are afraid of change, you do everything in your power to micromanage everybody and everything so things stay exactly the same.

Fear has turned us into control freaks.

Think about it. What is control? It's nothing more than a feeble attempt to protect ourselves from the chaos we imagine change will bring. You know you don't have the power to control the uncontrollable, but you still hang onto the illusion like a dog protecting his bone. I know I do it because there are times I'm afraid what will happen if I let go. It's important to remember control is merely a defensive behavior we use to manage our fear.

Here's the sobering reality: ***The only control you have is how you choose to react to change.*** Are you going to rise to the occasion or let it kick you in the butt? One thing is for certain-- change is constant. You can't stop it no matter how hard you try. So stop fighting it and make a conscious decision to switch gears just like Lisa did. We all have the power to enter the world of "everything's possible". We just have to want it badly enough.

Moving successfully through change comes down to asking yourself this very basic question: Do I deserve to be happy? A Real Cougar has no problem answering that question because she knows she is. At her core she is connected to a strong, unwaivering belief and sense of well being. She has an inner strength that let's her know she'll be okay no matter what. Even when she is going through her own personal Tsunami of Change down deep she knows she will get through it and be better for having had the experience. A Real Cougar will always look for and find a way to claim happiness.

You all know tsunamis are tremendously powerful and they can swamp your boat if you are not prepared. Tsunami waves are tricky because you don't know they're coming until they come crashing down on top of you. They start deep in your psyche and by the time they reach the surface it's too late to run for cover.

The Tsunami of Change is made up of little waves. Each one of those waves represent something in your past you weren't willing to deal with. You know what I'm talking about. The childhood scars, all the disappointments that were easier to sweep under the rug than to deal with. Those are the same scars that today make you eat too much, smoke too much, drink too much and have sex with the wrong people just to take away the emotional ache.

So far in my life I have experienced three major Tsunamis of Change. They hit full force at ages 19, 29 and 49. Each time it made me realize that the *pain of not changing was worse than the pain of staying the same.* At 19, it meant leaving home and moving to New York. At 29, it was learning how to start consciously creating my own circumstances and at 49, finding a way to reinvent myself and deal with my fear of aging. Any of those tsunamis could have swamped my boat, but I didn't allow that to happen. It's that spirit and determination that defines the Real Cougar.

Even now remembering those radical times of change is painful, but at the same time unbelievably healing. Do I expect another tsunami to hit someday? Absolutely, because like all of us I am still holding on to some painful issues that I am not yet prepared to deal with. Here's something I know for sure: One lifetime is not nearly enough time to fix everything. And, if there are times you delude yourself into thinking you have it all figured out, wait because another wave is on it's way. We are constantly evolving and that's a very good thing.

Here's the most important lesson my tsunamis have taught me: All of us women have to learn not to be so hard on ourselves. I don't know why but our attention also goes to the one thing we think we did wrong rather than the 100 things we did right. Isn't that crazy? We are actually choosing to feel bad. Remember that the next time you are raking yourself over the coals about some woulda, coulda, shoulda's and ask yourself, "Would I treat my best friend this way?" If the answer is no, take it easy. It's time to be your own best friend. Don't hold back. Treat yourself to the love and TLC you deserve.

Here's an analogy that makes it easier to understand tsunami's. In the middle of 2008 our economy started to go through its own destructive wave. Did it happen overnight? Of course not. There were warning waves everywhere, but nobody paid attention. It took a devastating crisis of confidence for the people in charge to take action. It's the same with us. *Sometimes it takes a crisis to get us to act responsibly and that's why I am learning to appreciate them.* I have said this before but it bears repeating. It takes the pain of not changing to become worse than the pain of staying the same. Now that you are thinking about it, isn't it amazing how long you allow your problems to fester before you do something about them?

All of us women have to learn not to be so hard on ourselves.

Real Cougars know there is no such thing as impossible. If we want something badly enough we are going to get it. We are going to find a way. Here's another great example of that.

Finding Her Voice

Robyn has a new dream at 53. In 2008, after nearly 30 years in public relations, she is pursuing her first love—acting! She had been a disc jockey for about five years after college and still volunteers at one of the NPR affiliate radio stations. Robyn's taking small steps in a new direction while still running her PR business. (Engaging in a part-time pursuit is a good way to test the waters before jumping in over your head).

Part of Robyn's new plan included finding an agent in order to ramp up her voiceover opportunities. She was nervous and unsure about how she would be received but that didn't stop her. One day she just walked into a local agency unannounced and told them what she wanted to do. She was shocked to find out there was a real demand for women over 40 who did voiceovers and they signed her immediately.

So far Robyn has been in a department store sales training film, three insurance company industrials, and has doubled her number of voiceover jobs. She is ecstatic and her renewed enthusiasm prompted her to sign up for a television acting class at a regional playhouse. Her next move is to audition for local community theater productions.

There is always a way to create your bliss if you want it badly enough. You can follow in the footsteps of Lisa and Robyn, but you do need to have to make several leaps of faith. That's where we are going next. I am going to explain my personal change model that contains 7 of the most crucial leaps. I call it "I CREATE". It's the solid foundation that makes all things possible. It has always worked for me and for all the successful women I have coached. Learn it, use it, believe in it and you'll will find out for yourself how amazing it is.

Chapter Three

"I CREATE"
Your Success Magnet

There's a pretty good chance if you're reading this book you've come to a crossroads in your life. You think you are ready to start moving from where you are now to where you want to go next, but you are still afraid. Even though you've come to the realization that happiness deserves a higher ranking on your priority list, thinking about change still gives you a queasy feeling in the pit of your stomach.

To get over being afraid of change you have to face it head on. To get what you want, you have to explore your possibilities, give up clinging to feeling comfortable and get it touch with what really turns you on. There are no shortcuts. You really do have to leap into the deep end of the pool. In fact, there are *seven leaps* you must take to become a master at creating what you want. I'll share them all in this chapter.

To get over being afraid of change you have to face it head on.

But for a lot of you this big leap approach may not compute. You have always been told to take small, comfortable baby steps to get where you are going. The flaw in that approach is you don't see enough tangible results to build the momentum that keeps you going. And the truth is, if you are not motivated by the results you will stop trying.

To change it is imperative that you forget what you've been told in the past and start with a clean slate. Find out from your own experience what works best for you. That's the only logical way you are going to grow and your future is in your hands. Always keep in mind, *it's not about the cards you're dealt– it's how you play your hand.*

Change is constant – we've already established that. What we want out of life keeps evolving. Relationships change, careers change, our beauty and our body are changing, and our financial base goes up and down like a yo-yo as well. Real Cougars know that ultimately the quality of our lives is a reflection of how well we handle change. The real challenge is how do you stay ahead of the curve with all the changes going on? This is how. You must set up a system that allows you to create the change you want and make it through the changes you have no control over. The "I CREATE" model, what I call your Success Magnet, is that system.

Real Cougars know that ultimately the quality of our lives is a reflection of how well we handle change.

Right now would be a good time to debunk another myth. I love doing that. This myth is don't assume you have to be ready for change before you make it. In reality, the only thing that convinces the brain that it's okay to change is to experience the changes. Realize change isn't as horrible as you imagine. In fact, change is your friend - not your enemy. It challenges us by putting us in situations that allow us to explore all our possibilities.

I get emails and phone calls every day from women who have made monumental changes in their *Don't assume you* lives. It runs the gamet - every- *have to be ready for* thing from winning their battles *change before you* with cancer, choosing passion over *make it.* security, starting their own businesses, divorcing and, yes, dating younger men. Are there times they're scared to death of change? You bet, but they move through the fear and do what they know they must do to feel good again. They are willing to do anything and everything it takes to get what they want. And now you will be too. "I CREATE" will help you.

It's really important to think long and hard about what you want for yourself. I remember these lines Robert Redford's character spoke in the movie *Out of Africa*. "I don't want to live someone else's idea of how to live. Don't ask me to do that. I don't want to find out one day that I'm at the end of someone else's life". Not being the person you were meant to be is a very scary proposition isn't it? That's what happens when your life is centered on making other people happy.

I fully understand this trepidation you feel about change. Just know we have all been in your shoes. Every woman on the planet goes through times of uncertainty. Every woman has those horrible episodes of overwhelm, when she believes she has run out of choices. It's during these times that our ability to change seems as unrealistic as the man in the moon. That's why this chapter of the book is so very important for all of us. Unleashing your Real Cougar is going to open you up to new possibilities. It did for me and thousands of other women who have taken the leap. Now it's your turn to find out exactly what you are made of.

There is one more thing I want you to be aware of before taking your big first leap. This change you are about to make is going to ruffle the feathers of those around you. Just think about it for a minute. These people have grown comfortable with you just the way you are. Your behavior has become safe and predictable. You being you doesn't threaten their well being. But when they sense even the smallest indication that you are changing they get nervous. Whether it's your mate, your kids, your friends, your extended family or your boss, they will be wondering how this new woman will affect them and your relationship with them. Please don't let that deter you. Being a Real Cougar has rewards you can't imagine until you start experiencing them for yourself. And if these people love you they will just have to get over their own insecurities and step up to the plate. And, guess what? They won't realize it, but your changes, your growth is going to help them too. That's what I call a win-win situation.

This change you are about to make is going to ruffle the feathers of those around you.

The "I CREATE" Model

Okay, it's time to get started. These are the seven leaps that are necessary to unleash your Real Cougar. This formula is your own personal Success Magnet. When you learn how to use it there isn't anything you won't be able to create. We are going to examine each leap one by one. The more you use your Success Magnet the faster you transition into the Real Cougar you know you are and always wanted to be.

YOUR SUCCESS MAGNET

"I" is for Imagination

"C" is for Choice

"R" is for Role Play

"E" is for Education

"A" is for Action

"T" is for Time-Out

"E" is for Endurance

Keep in mind the Real Cougar is multi-dimensional. She has five separate components – wellness, beauty, relationship, finance and spirituality. "I CREATE" insures that each of these areas are functioning well on their own while at the same time supporting each other-- just like that string of Christmas tree lights.

The First Leap – Imagination

Thank goodness for our imagination. It lifts our spirit and keeps our creative juices flowing. Without our imagination, life wouldn't be worth living. But, sometimes it doesn't matter how intent you are about being upbeat, you get weighted down in a routine that leaves you little time for yourself or your dreams. Each day becomes all about getting things done, not enjoying what you are doing. This is what happens when you spend too much in your head and not enough in your heart. Getting out of my head is something I work on every day.

The sad fact of the matter is, the more time you spend in your head, the greater the chance of developing the "what is" mentality. What is – "what is"? It's when you believe what you see today, what you saw yesterday and what you envision for tomorrow is all there is. It's thinking that is the direct opposite of anything's possible. Anything's possible is where you are headed now. That's the glorious place your imagination takes you when you give it the

The more time you spend in your head, the greater the chance of developing the "what is" mentality.

chance. It's the place of feeling good and that's where you need to be for any positive change to take place.

What are the old beliefs that have you stuck in the "what is"? Is it thinking you're too old to change, not smart enough to change, not strong enough to change, or clueless about the changes you want to make? Whatever has got you buffaloed, it's time to get rid of those energy sucking demons once and for all. It's time to stoke the fires of your imagination.

Right now go get a pencil and a piece of paper and write down three things you have always wanted. Imagine there is a handsome genie standing right in front of you. He is a 7-foot-tall, bare-chested guy wearing gold shoes with turned up toes. He tells you he is ready and able to grant your three wishes right here right now. If you are having trouble coming up with your wishes, don't be upset. Sometimes it takes a while for them to surface because you have stuffed them down very deep for a very long time.

I am telling you that everything you have ever wanted is still part of you. As you get quiet, as you get out of your head they will come flooding back.

Ask yourself what is that fire in my belly that just won't go away? What are the yearnings that arise in the quiet of the night? What are the things you haven't done that you regret the most? Be specific because now it's time to turn that pain into an awesome dream of what can be.

When you've chosen your top three, begin to picture them as if they were already a part of your life. What does each one look like? Do you see yourself getting dressed in your favorite designer suit and running out the door to the job of your dreams? Do you see yourself on your comfy sofa in front of a roaring fire with your head resting on the shoulder of the love of your life? Do you see yourself smiling because you have a million dollars in your bank account? Do you see yourself taking a dip in your fabulous pool? Our imagination is an ever ending resource and it's where manifesting begins.

Now that you have picked your top three, I want you to narrow that down to your number one pick. What do you want the most right now? Got it? This is the "anything's possible" that you are going to focus on throughout this chapter. When you go through the "I CREATE" formula this is the brass ring you will be reaching for. This is what you are going to create for yourself.

From Imagination to Reality

It's very important to be very clear and to provide as much detail as possible about your "anything's possible". See it, feel it, touch it, be one with it. To illustrate how that works I will share how my imagination made it possible for me to create my what can be which happened to be my dream apartment.

Living in New York City is great. I am lucky enough to be on the 32nd floor of a building that provides south, east and west vistas of this marvelous town. I never get tired of looking out and seeing the magnificent view. At night I feel like I am in an airplane looking down at all the twinkling lights.

When I moved into this brand new building in the late 70's, my apartment was referred to as a junior two. That meant it had one full bedroom and bathroom, a living room, small kitchen and a tiny second bedroom with powder room. I ended up using the second bedroom as a makeshift attic. I kept stuffing it with everything I didn't know what to do with. I am a neat freak so at least the clutter was hidden from view.

Well, as the years passed the makeshift attic couldn't hold another thing. And, in addition to that I had clothes hanging on my doorknobs because there was no room left in the closets. This was making me crazy and so I started a search for a new apartment. I had no trouble finding larger space, but they were either too expensive or too dark. Nothing matched my views and the sunlight that streamed through my windows all day long. I really didn't want to give that up.

During this two year process of push and pull between more space and giving up what I already had, the strangest thing happened. I started having recurring dreams about finding a magic door in my apartment and it led to more rooms I didn't know I had. I must have had this dream at least two dozen times, and so it forced me to pay attention. After thinking a lot about it, this is the conclusion I came to: I would stay in my apartment and break through the walls. There was only one problem with that dream-- people were living in the apartments I wanted.

But being a Real Cougar, I didn't let that stop me. One night I knocked on the door of my neighbors next door and across the hall. I announced I would be interested in buying their apartment. They must have thought I was nuts but they listened to me anyway. Of course, neither one of them had any intention of moving any time soon. I said, "That's okay," and gave each one a bid just in case they changed their minds.

About two months after that night, I ran into my neighbor who lived next door. He was a young single guy and he told me he was getting married and was going to move. I couldn't believe it. One down, one more to go.

Another 3 months passed and after returning from a weekend get-away there was a message on my answering machine. It was the sister of the man who lived across the hall. She told me her brother had passed away and while looking through his papers she had found my bid and wanted to sell! Now I have three apartments – my original and two more. The magic door I had dreamed about so often was now a reality. I got everything I wanted – more room with the same beautiful views. I am still living in my dream apartment and every time I walk through the front door and see the sun streaming through my windows, I feel blessed.

That's just one example what the power of imagination can do. There's nothing stopping your imagination from running wild but you. Never underestimate what you are capable of.

I would like you to be clear about your number one wish before you continue reading. Write down every detail. As of right now you are going to start living your life as if that thing – that special dream – has already come true. When you feel you are ready to do that then proceed to Leap Two.

Leap Two - Choice

Choice is the thing that determines the quality of our lives. We get to choose everything. I know sometimes you don't feel like you have that option, but you really do. Every day you have the freedom to choose whether to feel good or feed bad, grateful or ungrateful, abundant or poor, lucky or unlucky and worthy or unworthy. You get to choose whether the glass is half full or half empty. Every day you get to choose how you want to see your world.

You get to choose what to do with that fire in your belly. You get to choose what to do with that gnawing feeling that screams there is a lot more to you than you realize. Know this. You are capable of being whomever you | *Every day you get to* choose to be. You just have to want | *choose how you want* it badly enough. And, just so we're | *to see your world.* clear, every woman has a fire in her belly. Many are just too afraid to step into the heat.

You are responsible for your choices but taking responsibility for them is hard. That's why you are constantly hearing people say - "I didn't have a choice in the matter". Nothing could be further from the truth. Each one of you is going to make a gazillion choices throughout your lifetime. Some will be as trivial as choosing between a chocolate or a strawberry ice cream cone and some will be as crucial as picking the right mate. What you are thinking, how you really feel about yourself will always determine how you choose.

There are four big reasons why we choose badly.

1. Bad Thinking. You allow your thoughts to get stuck on the things you don't like, instead of the things that make you feel good. My suggestion is to stop whatever you are doing a few times each day and think about what you are thinking about. Ask yourself, "Are these thoughts productive or destructive? Do I feel good thinking these thoughts or do I feel bad thinking these thoughts?" This will give you some insight into how your thoughts are influencing your choices.

I have been monitoring my thoughts for so many years now it has become automatic and often mystifying. There are days when everything I am doing is working out perfectly and somehow I will get stuck thinking about the one thing that went wrong. I am, of my own free will, choosing to make myself feel bad. When I catch myself choosing bad thoughts I stop, switch gears and find a better thought. It works and you need to do it.

2. Excuses and Self-Imposed Limitations. Excuses will cripple you and severely limit what you are more than able to accomplish right now. Excuses stop your brain from thinking constructively. They prevent you from coming up with a positive working plan. They become your safety net – but this net has huge holes that make it easy to fall flat on your face.

Here are *the most common excuses women use to get off the hook.* How many of these are in your defensive arsenal?

> I'm not ready yet
>
> I'm not qualified
>
> I don't have time
>
> I'm overwhelmed
>
> I can't afford it

These five excuses will prevent you from ever discovering breakthrough solutions. Choose to get rid of them right now.

3. The Fear Factor. Any choice we make that is based in fear is a wrong choice. Fear, like excuses, keeps us stuck in the "what is". You have conditioned yourself to believe it's easier and safer to deal with what you know than to venture into the unknown. Fears and excuses are partners. When you are afraid you know you can come up with a million and one excuses not to do something. We rarely admit to ourselves or to anybody else that we're afraid, so we make excuses. When you unleash your Real Cougar, the fear factor is going to greatly diminish. I won't say it goes away completely, but it won't stop you dead in your tracks any more. You will move through it a lot quicker because you know you are strong enough to withstand anything life has to throw at you.

4. Hate To Say No. Women make bad choices because they don't know how to say no. They buy into the hype that putting their wishes first automatically makes them selfish. The word selfish has stopped smart women dead in their tracks for far too long. Here's the thing about selfish. When someone else labels you selfish, it's how they manipulate you into doing things their way. Don't buy into it! Stop allowing yourself to be pulled down by other people's misguided ideas of just what selfish is. Remember if there is no juice left in your battery you can't energize yourself or anyone else. Women are nurturers. We want to help others, but we need to be there to nurture ourselves first. That's not being selfish – it's just a fact of life.

Kate's Choice

Last year Kate got dumped by her husband of three decades. He chose to kick her to the curb for a perky thirty-something. When Kate got over the initial shock she realized she had choices. She could have fallen apart or she could choose to lose forty pounds, cut her hair, land a terrific job and purchase a dreamy little condo. Sounds like a no-brainer right?

Kate thought so too. Today she is loving her new life, and here's the icing on the cake—her ex husband is admitting he made a mistake and is begging her to take him back! She is choosing not to. She was not rescued by a Fairy Godmother and she did not win the lottery. Kate simply chose to improve her life. She didn't allow bad thinking, fear, excuses or the word "no" to hold her hostage.

Now is the time to take a good look at your life. There is no better way to see the results of the choices you have made up until now.

Leap Three - Role-Playing

Okay, you have let your imagination run wild and have come up with the one most exciting thing you want to create for yourself. You are starting to see more clearly how your life is a reflection of your choices. Now it's time to talk about the next leap in the "I CREATE" formula which is role playing.

Fake It 'Til You Make It

At the beginning, while you are still a cougar-in-training, it helps to engage in some role-playing. This will take you from the comfort of the "what is" to the more challenging world of "anything's possible". It will stretch you and get you thinking like the Real Cougar you want to unleash.

It's funny. As I'm writing about role-playing an episode of the TV show *Seinfeld* comes to mind. George, who always ends up with the short end of the stick, chooses to do exactly the opposite of what he would normally do. Instead of ordering a tuna fish sandwich he orders chicken salad. Instead of lying to impress a woman he tells the truth. For one day he did everything different. And, with the magic of television, the transformation of Old George into New George was knocking 'em dead! That's what you have to do. Leap out of your old persona and leap into the new and improved version of yourself.

Scientists tell us that learning involves physical changes in the brain. Eric R. Kandel, received the Nobel Prize in Medicine in 2000 for his pioneering work in this area. They conclude that our brains are constantly changing automatically as we learn. What does that mean? There's a huge difference between conceptual learning and mastering a new skill. It's the difference between knowing how to do something and being able to do it routinely and comfortably. In our lives, we can't reinvent our behavior every time we need to get something done. We have to rely on ingrained behavior patterns. Our challenge is to replace well-established problem behavior patterns with more effective ones.

Yes, it is realistic to believe you can change. You can jump over to a new life line, just as I did. New patterns can replace old ones. If you replace an old behavior with a more effective one, the newly ingrained pattern will virtually become permanent over time.

As you start to unleash your Real Cougar, don't get discouraged. Just be aware of what your old beliefs created for you and be determined to create something different. Be like George... make it a game so you don't even realize you are leaping out of your comfort zone. Ask yourself, "Who is the woman I want to become? And what am I willing to do differently to create her?"

You can start by determining what this new version of you should look like. When you look in the mirror now do you see that woman or do you need a makeover? Are you dressing for success? Are your hemlines too short or too long? Do your necklines plunge a little too far? Is your hair and makeup the best choice for a woman your age? Are you clothes too tight? Do you need to get in shape? Make no mistake all of these things matter. Remember, the package you present is very important. You want to turn heads of any man at any age with your look, your intelligence, your confidence and your sensuality. The outer package has to reflect what's going on the inside.

Ask yourself, "Who is the woman I want to become? And what am I willing to do differently to create her?

Next, choose a role model that has already achieved what you're after. Ask yourself, "What was this person willing to do that up to now you were not?" You've heard there are no free lunches, and that's true. In order to pursue a dream it's realistic to think your life is going to change. Successful people will be the first to tell you that having everything you want all at the same time is almost impossible. There is always going to be a push and pull going on inside of you. But, that's not a bad thing. It's great you're always going to have another dream to go after.

When you are looking around for the right role model you will see that successful people possess many of the same traits. Of course, it's important that you be specific about what your definition of success is. It's different for all of us but take a look at my criteria and perhaps it will help you figure out what's most important for you.

1. Knowing how to create what you want
2. Feeling good about who you are
3. Being fairly compensated for your efforts
4. Never forgetting how important it is to love and be loved
5. Be willing to help others

Successful people are willing to step out of their comfort zone and do battle with their fear. They are dreamers and they are creators. They work very hard. They know how important it is to surround themselves with people who have something to teach them. They have a strong spirit. They focus on what they have not what they don't have. They have an incredible amount of discipline and they are profoundly grateful for their gifts.

Always remember there are no limitations except the ones you impose upon yourself. If you have trouble seeing yourself as a smart and sexy temptress, imagine how a Real Cougar like Kim Cattrall or Halle Berry would go about seducing a man they found deliciously attractive. It's all right to copycat some traits you admire in someone else until you perfect your own set of skills.

I admit I was a copycat. My mentor was my boss. He had every-thing I wanted for myself. He was confident, smart, respected and rich. (At 29 I thought that's all it took to be happy). By following his lead it turbo-charged my career. Without his guidance I wouldn't have been successful in the totally male dominated industry I had chosen. But there is more than meets the eye in a good mentoring relationship. I remember when I did something that amazed even me, I couldn't wait to share it with him. Making him proud made my achievement even better.

The greatest two lessons my mentor taught me were:

> 1. Never think small
> 2. Always be secure with who I am

Oh, there's one more thing his support made me realize-- What a gift it is to give to someone else.

Now if you will allow me, I would love to be your mentor. I have so much to share with you.

Let me begin by asking you this: Do you have a goal? Do you know what you want for yourself? If you do, you are ahead of the game but if you have had trouble coming up with one, it's time to do it. To achieve any goal you need desire and a plan. The plan doesn't need to be set in stone, but it's an important element in keeping you on course.

Here's what I have found. If you wander too far off the main road, it's really hard to find your way back to center. That happens to me all the time. I call it being attracted to the next shiny object syndrome. That's why every once in awhile I have to reel myself back to center – to what's most important. That's why you need a plan. Keep your mind on the prize and never doubt you are going to capture it. That's key!

I was a late bloomer. Setting up goals and plans didn't begin until I was 29. My first goal was to work in the trading department and my second was to make a lot of money. It was no accident that these goals rose to the top of the heap. You see ever since I was a young girl, it was very important that I was financially secure. I got that from my father – you see there is always a benefit to be found if you are willing to look for it.

I wanted to be independent, never having to rely on anybody to provide what I couldn't provide myself. When other teenagers were out spending their allowances mine was going into a savings account. We all have different things to work out so don't judge your goals or even try to figure them out, just accept them as unfinished business that needs to be worked out.

Making goals feel real is important. Here's something I did to make my mine more tangible. I sat down and made a projection of what I wanted to earn in the next ten years. I allowed myself to dream and the dream was a big one. At the time, the numbers I wrote down seemed like utter fantasy, but thinking about them made me very happy. Over the years I kept all doubt away from my dream. And because I did that the universe conspired with me to make it come true. Ten years later when I looked at those projections, they were almost a perfect match to what

I actually had earned. That's why I am such a huge fan of role play or fake it 'till you make it.

Leap Four – Education

In order to successfully create something new, you need to find something beneficial to replace the old. If you don't take the time to do this, you will keep sliding back to your bad habits. Education is how you find the something new. Education is how you formulate a plan. Education is where you learn strategy. Education is where you realize you cannot do it alone. Education gives you structure.

Success is never on sale. It doesn't come from waiting for miracles. You are the miracle. *You have to make it happen. Invest your time and your dollars in yourself.*

Your role models and mentors are always searching for new ways to take themselves to the next level. They have figured out that if you are standing still, you are really moving backward. If you don't follow through, there will always be someone else who will. Nobody is always successful—life is packed with hills and valleys. You just want to make sure you don't stay in the valley too long.

In 2004 Tiger Woods made a number of changes to his swing. He felt he was in a valley. He wanted to make the world's best golf swing even better. It took him a year to work out the kinks but he didn't get discouraged taking the time to learn something new. It paid off because in 2004 he won his fourth Masters, The

British Open and placed second in the U.S. Open. Those wins translated into $10 million in winnings. I'd say he made a wise decision, wouldn't you?

Success is never on sale. It doesn't come from waiting for miracles. You are the miracle. No matter what you are planning to create, you need the help of someone who has already arrived where you want to go. Education and the support it offers is a very important part of the "I CREATE" formula. It really does take more than the dream. Becoming a Real Cougar Woman involves learning some new skills, just like Tiger did. And, just like Tiger it will take a little while to work out the kinks, but the juice is going to be well worth the squeeze.

You have spent some time and have come up with a goal. Whatever it is, you have to learn everything you can about how to achieve it. My goal is to make The Real Cougar Woman a movement that empowers women all over the world. Do I think that it's possible? Of course I do, but I also realize I require a lot more learning to make that happen. I am the locomotive running my train. It's not going to be pull out of the station unless I provide the fuel.

When I first started The Real Cougar Woman, I didn't have a clue of how to make it successful. Remember my background was on Wall Street, so I knew absolutely nothing about the internet, blogging, writing, marketing, publicity or sales. And, mark my words, I have learned how important all those things are from all the mistakes I have made. Those mistakes, even though they didn't seem like it at the time, were really blessings. They made it very obvious that I needed to go out and get myself a first rate education on how to run a small business.

Realizing you need help is key. Support can make all the difference. Whether it's help in running your business, moving ahead in your corporate job, or finding the right guy, the willingness to admit you need help will help make the dream a reality. Often all you need is one gem of an idea to help you turn the corner.

Leap Five - Action

Up to this point, everything you have done was in preparation for this moment. You have used your imagination to pick your dream. You are starting to realize why you make the choices you do. You see how important it is to have a role model and it's okay to fake it 'till you make it. You understand why education and support are so necessary in making your dream real. So, now it's time to leap out of your comfort zone. It's time to push out the walls, crash through the ceiling and turn the theoretical into the tangible.

This is the only way you are going to get rid of your training wheels and put your new "I CREATE" model to the test. Yes, Cougars-in-Training it's time for action. Time to take a giant leap and start consciously creating what you want. This is where the wannabe's separate themselves from the achievers. You are an achiever.

It's time to push out the walls, crash through the ceiling and turn the theoretical into the tangible.

Remember, think big. That first leap needs to give you a burst of energy that will keep the momentum going. Believe in what you are doing and have the courage of a Real Cougar to follow through. That's the only way you are going to find out what you are capable of doing.

Lilly Ledbetter knows that better than anyone. For 10 years after she took an early retirement in 1998 she fought for what she knew was right. This grandmother from Alabama made it all the way to The White House making it better for all women, even though it would be too late for her to benefit personally.

In 1979 Lilly began work at the Goodyear Tire and Rubber Company in Gadsden, Alabama. During her years as a salaried worker at this factory, raises were given and denied based on evaluations and recommendations regarding worker performance. All merit increases had to be substantiated by a formal evaluation. In March 1998, Ledbetter inquired into the possible sexual discrimination of the Goodyear Tire Company Here's why. She started with the same pay as a man but by retirement, she was earning $3,727 per month compared the fifteen men who earned anywhere from $4,268 to $5,236 doing the exact same job.

In July she filed charges with The Equal Employment Opportunity Commission. In November 1998, Lilly sued claiming pay discrimination under Title VII of the Civil Rights Act of 1964 and the Equal Pay Act of 1963. In 2007 The Supreme Court ruled against her in a 5-4 decision.

Now almost 2 years later, on January 29th, 2009 President Obama signed the Lilly Ledbetter Fair Pay Act into law reversing the Supreme Court's ruling. This means everyone who is a victim of wage discrimination can hold their employer accountable. Isn't that a remarkable achievement? I am sure there were times Lilly wanted to call it quits, but she didn't. What a great role model for all of us.

Taking action is all about confronting your fears, and that's why it can make you want to run away and hide. However, a Real Cougar doesn't allow unrealistic boogey men to keep her from moving ahead. Here's what I have found every time I take action. The reality is never as scary as the terrifying scenario I concocted in my head.

Every year when it came time to negotiate my compensation package I would be nervous as hell. It didn't matter how many times I did it, my knees would feel like jello and I would break out in a cold sweat. My boss, even though he was my mentor, was a force to be reckoned with. He was tough and he was smart and could work you over better than anyone I know. Even though I did my research and prepared my pitch with precision, I knew he would make me work hard to get what I wanted. There were years that I won my battle and got more than I ever expected and there were years I had to settle for less. But you know what? Even when I didn't get everything I asked for I felt so proud of myself for stepping into the lion's den. I had many male partners who didn't have the courage I did.

Would it have been easier not to negotiate and just accept what he decided to give me? At first blush, you might say of course it would. But, that's not what happens. If you don't make the effort you'll never know what could have been if you had. I never want to live with regret. In my book, that's a lot worse than failing.

It gets a lot easier to take action when you adopt the philosophy that there are no such things as mistakes. I look at my not so terrific outcomes as matches that will ignite new ideas. Failure stretches your imagination and helps you create a new and better way. Knowing what doesn't work – you shift gears and try something different. You never know what's going to create the magic until you give it a whirl.

Leap Six – Time Out

Are you starting to feel a little overwhelmed with everything you need to do to create what you want? Don't worry – it's a natural reaction. That's why it's essential to make a "time out" part of your new routine – and not just today, but every day. You need to give your brain a rest, get quiet, take a deep breath and unwind. It's during this precious "you" time that your most creative ideas will take form.

Time out is when you get answers from your broader perspective. It's taking you away from the "what is" and allowing you to feel the joy of the "what can be". During this private time don't get caught up in the how-to's, simply focus on your intention. Leap into this broader part of who you really are and allow the natural expansion to take place.

Time out's look different to every woman. For some it might be a 20 minute meditation, taking a yoga class, getting a massage, engaging in a sexual fantasy or just lying down and listening to your favorite CD. You know what works for you. And if you don't, try them all until you find out. You'll know when you hit the bulls eye because your energy will be restored and you will have new ideas to explore. It's amazing what a little R&R will do for your creativity gene.

Now that your day includes periodic "how do I feel checkups" you will have no trouble determining when it is time to take a pause that refreshes, even if it's just five minutes at work.

I am sure you know firsthand that when you feel overwhelmed, angry, frustrated, vindictive, sad, underappreciated – it's impossible to create what you want. When you are feeling bad and

Time out is when you get answers from your broader perspective.

still push to get things done, things go from bad to worse. That is why Real Cougars intercept these negative emotional missiles that threaten their day by creating a safe place to regroup.

I want you now to create your very special Time-Out and start to incorporate it into your daily plan.

Leap Seven – Endurance

This last leap is just as important as the first. In fact, without it your Success Magnet won't have enough power to pull you toward the rewards you are looking for. If you are anything like me you love when a plan comes together and you get instant gratification. Sure, that happens on occasion, but it's not realistic. The more likely scenario is it will take time for a well-designed plan to start yielding results. It's during this lag time that things can get dicey. You get impatient and start making excuses of why it's not going to happen. Don't fall into that trap. You have put in too much time and effort to not go the distance.

Ask any successful person you know if they were an overnight sensation. Most likely that will make them laugh. To outsiders it may appear to be that easy, but actually it has taken years of honing their skills to make it to the top. They had a passion and they had the endurance to tough it out. I want you to do the same thing.

I wrote earlier in the book how important it is to start living your life as if the thing you want the most is already here. That's the bet way I know to go the distance.

Ask any successful person you know if they were an overnight sensation. Most likely that will make them laugh.

Here's a fabulous example of how that works.

Peggy's Vision

Peggy McColl, is a New York Times bestselling author. Of course she didn't start her writing career topping the bestseller list - it took passion, talent and endurance. She knew the importance of remaining positive throughout the manifestation process and not allowing the waiting process to get her down. Here are four different strategies she incorporated into her everyday life that helped her stay excited and upbeat.

First, she went online and printed a copy of The New York Times bestseller list. Then she added her book title, put it in a small Plexiglas card and kept it by her bed. Can't you just feel how jubilant she felt every single time she looked at it?

Second, she brought home a giant rawhide dog bone and wrote "I am a New York Times Bestselling Author" all over it. It was a reminder to hold onto her dream like a dog holds onto its bone.

Third, she pulled out her copy of Robert Kiyosaki's, block-buster Rich Dad, Poor Dad and cut off the starburst with the gold emblem that signified it was a New York Times Bestseller. She then pasted it on the back cover of her book Your Destiny Switch. But, that's not all. Peggy then headed over to Office Depot and made color copies of her "cut and paste" creation and put them up all over her house. And, finally she sent a copy to other people so they would get on board with her dream. Collective energy flowing in the right direction really does speed up the manifestation process.

And, finally Peggy let her imagination run wild. Putting on her baseball cap and sunglasses she headed off to the grocery store. She imagined she was a famous New York Times Best Selling Author who was trying to hide her identity from adoring fans clamoring for an autograph. Like I have said throughout this book—do whatever it takes!

I don't have to tell you that it wasn't long after using all of these visualizations that Peggy's dream became her reality. You see how important it is to incorporate and maintain a strong, vivid belief system. It's how you endure the waiting time, the time when most people get discouraged, that can either speed up your "I CREATE" magnet or send you back to square one.

Now that you have read all Seven Leaps go back and read them again and again. Cut them out and put them by your bed, on your refrigerator, in your bathroom, and on your desk. "I CREATE" is your Personal Success Magnet and the more you use it the more powerful it becomes.

One thing I want to make perfectly clear. I would never ask you to do anything that I haven't done myself. Using "I CREATE" has made such a positive difference in my life. In fact, I am using every leap in the creation of this book.

Some of the changes you will see are subtle, but don't underestimate their power. In six months when you look back to where you were and compare it to where you are now, it's going to totally amaze you.

Chapter Four
Staying Ahead Of
The Aging Curve

There are a few things in life that are undisputable and here's one of them: When you're not feeling up to snuff, everything else gets relegated to the back burner. When your back is aching, your nose is running, your stomach is crampy or your head is pounding, all your thoughts are focused on one thing and one thing only and that's feeling better.

It's funny how you expect your body to perform without a hitch even when you are constantly abusing it   Well, that might work in your 20's or even your 30's but once you turn 40 things are going to change.   Your body is your temple, so from now on start treating it with the respect it deserves.

Ask any woman what she likes about her body and she will turn the question around and tell you what she doesn't like. She might be a pear shape and wants to be an apple, she wants to drop 10 pounds, have a flatter stomach, she detests her cellulite and stretch marks, her breasts are either too small or too large and the list goes on and on. You never hear – I love my body just the way it is and I am so grateful it works so beautifully.

Well, don't you think it's time more of you started to appreciate what you've got?

We've already established that change is constant and even though you may not want to accept it, your body is making some pretty major changes with each passing decade. How well you take care of yourself now will set

Ask any woman what she likes about her body and she will turn the question around and tell you what she doesn't like.

the tone for how well your body performs in the future. Just like your car, the more miles it logs the more TLC it requires. To stay fit, vibrant and strong I recommend more frequent tune-ups and higher grade fuel. That means different nutritional supplements, new diagnostic tests, better quality diet and age appropriate exercise routines. Respect your body so it does not become the unhappy victim of benign neglect.

Nutritional Supplements is one the ways I take care of my body and boost its efficiency. I must take over 30 capsules every day. I didn't start doing that until I was 50 but now it's become a

Your body is making some pretty major changes with each passing decade.

ritual. My newest discovery in the world of vitamins comes from a company called GeneWize. They have actually found a way to custom blend supplements to match

your DNA. Pretty cool don't you think?

When you place your first order, the company sends you everything you need to swab a DNA sample which you then send back to them. Once they receive it they analyze it and then according to your particular deficiencies they custom blend your supplements and mail them back to you. You will also receive a copy of their DNA evaluation and a breakdown of all the ingredients that are in your daily capsules.

I was skeptical at first, wondering if this was something that would really work or just another sales promotion. I was pleasantly surprised! Since I have been taking my GeneWize supplements I have been sleeping better, my migraine headaches seem to have vanished and even my chronic constipation is no longer a problem. It's seems like a mini miracle, and I'm thrilled with the results.

The Healthy Cougar Lifestyle

Of course you can't start a good health regime without incorporating good diet and exercise habits. Talk to any doctor worth their salt and they will tell you that proper food and physical activity have the biggest impact on how you age. Yes, my Real Cougars it's 80% lifestyle 20% genetics, but you knew that already. No free lunches!

By the way, I can't talk about what I eat these days without paying homage to Trader Joe's. When they opened their first store in Manhattan just a few blocks from my apartment, I couldn't run there fast enough. I am trying my best to eat more organic foods and this store is making it a lot easier to do that. Of course, cooking your own meals is always preferable, but when you are pressed for time reaching into your freezer for a healthy entrée is a good alternative to pizza or Chinese food. I love their products. In fact just writing about it is making me hungry! My downfall is ice cream. Chocolate ice cream seems to soothe my soul and makes the world a better place. I admit I treat myself more often than I should. But like everything else in life, if you maintain an overall healthy balance you'll be just fine.

It's impossible to achieve a healthy balance without bringing up the subject of exercise. I know it's tough finding the energy and the time to work out but you have to do it. Most weeks I hit the gym three times and here's the simple routine I follow.

30 Minutes of Cardio – I like the elliptical. It's easier on your knees than running on the treadmill. I vary my cardio by either maintaining a constant elevated heart rate for 30 minutes or interval training where the heart rate fluctuates. The purpose of interval training is to give your metabolism a jumpstart which of course burns more calories.

60 Minutes with Fred, my trainer - That workout includes 30 minutes of stretching and 30 minutes of weight bearing exercises. It's imperative that you keep your bones strong and these exercises can actually reverse the natural loss that occurs with aging.

Walking – Incorporate more walking into your daily routine. Also, take the stairs rather than the elevator. These little changes can make a big difference in how you burn calories and develop muscle.

Am I one of those women who love to exercise? Hell no! I can think of a million things I would rather be doing with that time. I work out because I know I have to do it to fight the aging process. I don't want to be one of those frail old ladies who struggles just to step onto the bus. I see myself dancing at 95 with my 75 year old lover. Once you make exercise a regular part of your routine finding time to sweat does get easier. So whether it's at home, the gym or outside for a 30 minute power walk get moving.

Physically Speaking

Here's something else I do to insure my good health—I schedule yearly physical checkups. When you get into the habit of going once a year, it makes it easier for your doctor to notice small changes that might have occurred between visits. I devote the month of March to getting all of my checkups done.

> 8 Tests Every Woman Over 40 Needs To Take:
>
> 1. Yearly mammogram
>   (sonogram if you have dense breasts)
> 2. Yearly bone density
> 3. Yearly physical checkup
> 4. Yearly Pap Smear
> 5. Yearly Transvaginal Ultrasound
> 6. Yearly visit to your Dermatologist for skin cancer check
> 7. Yearly chest x-ray
> 8. Colonoscopy every 5 years

Just in case you're not familiar with the Transvaginal Ultrasound, here's the scoop. It's a test to check your ovaries, uterus and fallopian tubes for fibroids, tumors and other potential problems. A thin wand is inserted into your vagina and that's how they see a picture of what's going on inside. It's painless. All you have to do is lie there with your legs open and breathe.

Make sure you get your blood checked at least twice a year too. That includes getting a full hormone panel, thyroid panel, cholesterol panel & homocysteine check (which helps determine your risk for heart disease or stroke).

Oh, yes, can't forget this one last test – CA-125. This is recommended for any women with a family history of ovarian cancer or questionable symptoms such as change in bowel habits, fatigue, low back pain, loss of appetite or gastrointestinal upset. Just so you know many of these tests are not included in a routine blood test, but I recommend you ask for them.

Small lifestyle changes can pay big dividends for Real Cougars who choose to stay healthy and vibrant. According to John Morley, M.D. author of The Science of Staying Young, "Living well and feeling good enough to do whatever you want to do throughout your lifetime is priceless."

He suggests that little changes that can mean a lot and he wants to make it fun to stay young. Here are two of my favorite changes from Dr. Morley:

1. Eat a nutritious and balanced diet. Strive for 4 servings of fish a week and substitute fish oil capsules if you fall short. Enjoy moderate amounts of alcohol - a drink a day for women and, at most, two a day for men. Add plenty of fruits and vegetables, enough proteins and lots of fiber to keep things running smoothly.

2. Don't lose weight after age 60. Don't you love that one? Get in shape when you're younger by combining exercise and a healthy diet to build muscle. It's healthier to be "pear-shaped" and carry extra weight in your hips than be "apple-shaped" and have a larger waistline. "The good news is that as you get older, being slightly overweight may actually improve how long and well you live," Morley says. "Learn to love your slightly Rubenesque body." So eat your chocolate, drink your favorite wine and above all have fun. It could add years to your life.

The Sleep Factor

There's another thing that could add quality years to your life – getting enough sleep. The National Sleep Foundation reports that sixty percent of American women are not getting enough sleep. How many mornings do you wake up more exhausted than when you went to bed? Every woman I talk to is complaining she is always tired—so tired in fact that if there was a choice of more sleep or more sex, she is choosing more sleep.

When the going gets tough and all you want is a nap, do you just push on, often downing a cup (or three) of coffee to get through the day? And, when it is finally time to go to sleep you're so keyed up you can't. According to a poll (which surveyed 1,003 women between the ages of 18 and 64), women spend the last hour before bedtime watching television, doing household chores or working in front of a computer. All of these activities make it harder to fall asleep. The experts recommend dimming lights and avoiding stressful activities, including computers and television, for the last hour before bed.

I want to conclude this chapter with the personal story of Maryk Kohlman. Maryk is a member of my Real Cougar Woman Club and she graciously agreed to talk to me about the health challenge she is now facing. No woman should ever have to hear those dreaded words, "You have breast cancer," but Maryk did.

Maryk's Story

Every October the color PINK is plastered everywhere! Ribbons fly, we see bumper stickers on automobiles, kitchen accessories, and even M&Ms have a PINK coat on.

Pink used to be my favorite color, until September 2008 when I was diagnosed with Breast Cancer. After that I never wanted to see the color pink again. For me it was an in your face reminder that screamed, "You have cancer!" I gave away my pink sheets, pillows, jewelry, anything I owned that was pink, even my favorite jacket.

I couldn't believe this was happening to me. Here I was starting a new life. I had just started to date again after my divorce. I wanted my 50's to be my best years and all I could think about was who would want to be with me if I had cancer. I found that the men my own age would say, "Sorry to hear about that...keep in touch and let me know how you are doing." On the surface it sounds very polite, but for me, it was crushing—it meant they wanted to run away because I was no longer desirable.

Well, I must admit I was in for a big surprise. It didn't take long for my eyes and my heart to be open to a whole new generation of young people who were supportive, not judgmental, about what I was going through. When I said, "I have breast cancer", the younger guys would reply, "How do you feel and do you want to go out tonight?" I was so shocked at first. I thought maybe they didn't hear me correctly. I would say it again..."I have breast cancer. I had a tumor removed and I have a scar on my breast." They would say, "Oh really? I have some scars too" as they laughed our loud.

The younger men were not afraid of the word. Some of them shared their stories, about their own mothers having gone through it. I was amazed by their attitudes. Younger people see hope in the future, not defeat. They concentrate on the positive, they live in the moment. I remembered those feelings, from my younger days. Why is it that we stop living like that? I am not saying, we shouldn't be responsible, but sometimes we have to learn to fly by the seat of our pants. To take the risk, to one again believe in ourselves.

What I realized from all of this...is we are our own worst enemy... pointing out our faults for the world to critique. As my attitude changed about myself, others began to view me differently. The more I dated, the more confident I became with my looks, my age. my body and my scars.

Although, this time in my life has not been easy. my younger man has helped make my experience with breast cancer so much more tolerable. My focus has been on living my life, grabbing the gusto with grace. I made up my mind if I was going to be able to handle this, I had to forget about it and get out there and LIVE.

I am entering a new phase... I am living as a Real Cougar and loving it ! Oh by the way—I am wearing PINK again!

Chapter Five
How Hormonal
Hotties Stay Cool

Cougars, all of you are going to find out just what menopause is all about sooner or later. Whether you experience it naturally or feel the effects because of surgery or medication, I'm afraid there is no escape. If the hot flashes don't drive you nuts, then just realizing you are old enough to go through "the change" can do a real number on your psyche. But you know what? I think the "pause" in menopause is what it's all about. It's giving you a time-out to reflect on your life and think about what's next.

How you decide to handle "the pause" is going to affect every part of you—your skin, bones, heart and brain health, sexual desire, energy and your overall sense of well being. Now is the time you really have to start paying attention to the messages your body is constantly sending you, such as an ache that doesn't want to go away, waking up exhausted, frequent headaches, nausea, feeling bloated. You have to understand that your body is reeling from the turmoil that hormone imbalance causes.

Realizing you are old enough to go through "the change" can do a real number on your psyche.

It would be great if there was just one magic formula that was perfect for every woman's changing body. Unfortunately there is no such thing. We have many choices available to us – everything from hormone therapy to nutritional supplements. And that's where it gets really dicey, because it becomes your job to find out how to best get your hormones back into balance. What are you going to do to feel good and stay healthy for all the productive years that lie ahead?

Feeling the effects of my approaching menopause really put my third tsunami on the fast track. I wasn't happy about getting older and I imagine most of you aren't either. That's because the previous generations didn't set a very good example for us to follow. For me menopause was the red flag broadcasting that my best years were behind me. I couldn't shake that gnawing feeling of sadness which was only exacerbated by the prevailing Wall Street mentality that at 40 you were considered a dinosaur. So at 48 I felt like I already had one foot in the grave. Of course, now I realize that none of that hype was true, but when you hear the same song long enough you start to sing it yourself.

Weaving your way through the menopause maze today can be extremely challenging. There is so much information to absorb and so much contradiction that it's easy to become completely confused. It took me a year of total frustration and physical discomfort before I saw the light at the end of the tunnel. You need patience and perseverance. I made finding the right answers like a business and *I was the CEO in charge of my own body.* And, cougars I highly recommend that you do the same thing. You must be your own best health care advocate.

Kim's Take on Menopause

It's funny how we talk about life stages in negative terms in our culture. We talk about the terrible twos, the troubled teen years, and we all anticipate having a midlife crisis. I spent my younger years thinking that I would not be the person with the midlife crisis; that I would breeze through menopause and come out on the other side unscathed. Given that I walked away from a more than 20-year marriage and had been in a solid relationship with a much younger man for over three years now, some may say that I have had a major midlife crisis. I would disagree.

I think that there is a wisdom that comes with age. There's also a change in the amount of crap you are willing to tolerate as you get older. As Katharine Hathaway says, "The change of life is the time when you meet yourself at a crossroads and you decide whether to be honest or not before you die."

Then comes menopause. The whole menopause thing means that a phase of our lives as women is over and for many of us this was the phase that defined us. Feeling it coming to an end can feel like a crisis but I decided that there is another way to look at it. It came to me one day that these flashes of heat were not unlike the labor pains I experienced giving birth. Ok, so they didn't hurt nearly as much, but could be difficult and embarrassing. It was this realization that made me start to look at this whole menopause thing differently. I stopped looking at it as the ending of something and started to see it as a birth...the birth of a new, stronger, more confident me---the birth of my next phase of life. I breathed through each hot flash just as I had through each labor pain, knowing that in the end I would have an amazing new being. Only this time, the being would be me.

Menopause can be a beginning or an ending. It depends on how you view it. People can think I was having some sort of crisis when I left my marriage and moved on to my new relationship, but I know better. I'm having a midlife awakening...no crisis here.

Things you need to know

Finding a doctor you trust and respect during your hormonal transition is the most important piece of the menopause puzzle. Menopause is a long journey. Some women might tell you that it's no big deal, but it really is. It's not just about hot flashes and night sweats, it's about the major transition your body goes through before during and after menopause. You owe it to yourself to travel down this road with a partner who puts your best interests first. This means a physician who is competent, caring, and up on the latest cutting-edge information to help you navigate through that never-ending maze of information.

Roughly 13 years ago when I began my search for answers there wasn't a lot of discussion on the topic of menopause. It was hidden away in the closet because it was an embarrassment. You didn't even talk about it with other women.

To alleviate symptoms there was a one-size-fits-all protocol called Premarin. It was the drug of choice and that's what my doctor prescribed for me. Premarin did take away my symp-

Finding a doctor you trust and respect during your hormonal transition is the most important piece of the menopause puzzle.

toms but it also made me queasy and bloated so I stopped using it. When I asked for another treatment there was only silence because she really had no clue of what else to give me. I left that doctor and went on a search for another. That search took over a year and included trying different protocols with four different doctors. Then I found the right physician and the right therapy for me.

If you think you are ready to find a new doctor, follow your gut and do it. Ask your friends for a referral. If that doesn't work, check out The North American Menopause Society. They maintain referral lists on their website, www.menopause.org. for women in the United States and Canada who are searching for physicians.

Natural menopause begins with perimenopause. This is a six to eight year journey culminating in full-blown menopause. Perimenopause is the natural decline of estrogen and proges-terone levels in your body. Periods can become irregular and you may experience hot, flashes, night sweats, spotty periods, irritability, mood swings and brief episodes of memory loss that some of us call senior moments. Your body starts to lose its leanness and the area around your stomach becomes thicker.

The average age for menopause is 45 to 55 but for some women it can start earlier. In fact these days women are experiencing the symptoms in their late 30' due to of their extremely stressful lives. Stress affects hormone levels an awful lot. You are officially in menopause when you have not had a period for 12 months in a row.

If you have a hysterectomy and both your uterus and ovaries are removed you go into full blown menopause immediately.

Medical Records. When you first start to experience any of these changes it's important to go to your doctor and have your hormone levels checked. This is the perfect time to start a medical records file. Whenever you get a blood test, mammography, thyroid and hormone panel, bone density test ask for a duplicate copy of the results and stick them in your file. This gives you a benchmark to chart important changes as you age. Believe me this simple discipline will save you a lot of time and energy as you try to find the menopause protocol that works best for you.

Hormones are a chemical substance made by a gland or organ and it regulates your various body functions. They are very powerful, so never underestimate the havoc they can create. Your menopausal symptoms are the result of your body's hormonal imbalance. And, here's something important you need to remember—in fact, it will help you retain your sanity---your symptoms are very real, you are not imagining them. Never let anyone tell you you're over reacting. And trust me, they will try.

Symptoms

- Weight gain, especially around the belly

- Loss of sexual desire

- Hormonal headaches (migraines)

- Forgetfulness

- Depression and feeling a loss of control

- Weaker bones more susceptible to fracture

- Dryness of vaginal walls making intercourse painful

- Skin that becomes dry and less firm

- Collagen loss resulting in more lines, wrinkles
  and hollows

- Interrupted sleep patterns leaving you tired,
  moody and irritable

The Right Time To Start HRT (Hormone Replacement Therapy). There's a critical window of time for starting HRT. The women in the Women's Health Initiative 2002 Study (WHI) who were 20 years past menopause had a 71% higher risk of heart attack on estrogen and progesterone than those taking placebos, but women closer to menopause had an 11% lower risk of heart problems.

"HRT seems to help preserve thinking ability when started just after menopause, but it may hasten the progression of pre-existing memory problems when started later in life," writes JoAnn E. Manson, a Harvard Medical School professor who was a lead investigator on both the WHI and the long-running Nurses' Health Study.

HRT was associated with a lower risk of fractures and colorectal cancer regardless of age.

A growing number of experts now believe that the women in the WHI -- average age 63 -- do not reflect the typical women entering menopause, and that the same risks may not apply to younger women.

The HRT Debate. Although many experts dismiss "bio-identical" as a meaningless term, proponents use it to mean hormones with the same molecular structure as those that women's bodies make. Chemically equivalent estradiol is available in many FDA-approved pills, patches, creams and gels from traditional drug companies, generally made from the exact same plant sources that compounding pharmacies use. What's more, the FDA-approved varieties are covered by insurance, unlike compounded blends that can cost between $100 and $150 per month.

A growing number of doctors prescribe these estradiol-based products instead of Premarin, the estrogen made from horse urine that was used in the WHI study. Many also prefer natural progesterone, to the synthetic form that was used in the WHI.

Compouding Pharmacies

To get the exact dose of of homones your body is deficient in you need a physician to write a prescription for bioidentical hormones. That prescription is then filled by a compounding pharmacy.

FDA-approved products with estradiol & progesterone

If you go this route you will not get the exact amount your body requires, you will receive a prescription for the standard dose the pharmaceutical company manufactures.

Estradiol:

- Alora
- Vivelle
- Estrace

- Climara
- Estraderm
- Estrogel

Progesterone:

- Prometrium
- Crinone

How To Take Your Hormones:

Estradiol applied to the skin in patch, cream or gel form is preferable to oral consumption because it has been shown to lower the risk of blood clots and strokes. A large study in France published in the Lancet found that women taking estrogen in pill form were three times as likely to develop blood clots than non-users, while women using the estradiol patch had no increased risk. But more study is needed to determine this conclusively.

Progesterone is best taken in capsule form just before bedtime.

Increased Risk of Breast Cancer. The increased risk of breast cancer appears to be connected to progestin rather than estrogen. Women taking both estrogen and a synthetic form of progestin (synthetic-brand name Provera) in the WHI had eight more cases of breast cancer per 10,000 than the control group; women taking estrogen alone had six fewer cases. Women who still have a uterus need some progesterone to guard against uterine cancer, but many doctors now try to give the lowest dose possible to prevent a build-up of uterine lining.

Diet and Lifestyle Changes. The foods and nutrients we eat make up the building blocks for our hormones. For some women, adding more protein, high-quality fats, and fresh fruits and vegetables, while limiting refined carbohydrates, sugar, gluten, and highly processed foods can make a world of difference in their menopause experience.

Phytotherapy. Soy, black cohosh, red clover, Ashwagandha, wild yam — the list of plants nature provides for healing menopausal symptoms is lengthy and time-honored. You can choose to work with a practitioner to find the right plant-based combination for you, or explore an effective combination of herbs for the relief of menopausal symptoms.

My Protocol. I have chosen BHRT (bioidentical hormone replacement therapy). My estradiol and testerone is blended into a cream which I rub into the inside of my upper arm every morning. I also take progesterone in a capsule every night. I have been on this protocol for the past 12 years and have been very pleased with the results. I have no menopausal symptoms and am happy to say my health is excellent. After doing my own research I feel confident that this protocol not only eliminates menopausal symptoms but also protects my mind and body from the diseases directly related to aging.

The bioidentical testosterone in my protocol keeps my sex drive in high gear. Be sure to check with your physician about that, especially if you are noticing a decline in your sexual energy. Any deficit will become very apparent when reading your hormone panel.

So there you have it, everything you need to know about menopause. I urge you to read as much as you can about your changing body so when you visit your doctor you will be prepared to discuss all of your options.

Menopause is natures way of telling you to get off life's merry-go-round and start exploring new and fun ways to find happiness. It's the purr-fect time to re-discover the magnificent Real Cougar that you are.

Gladys' Story

Gladys' take: "Think very carefully before you say good-bye to the sex goddess that we all are. The choices you make when you start to feel the symptoms of menopause will determine how much fun you are going to have from now on. Do you want to be a Real Cougar or a let yourself morph into a sweat suit, sneaker wearing frump"?

Gladys remembers well how scary it was as a child to hear her mother speak of "IT", meaning menopause. She railed about the horrors of getting fat, sprouting facial hair and losing her sexual desire.

Her mother believed that when her vagina got dry she would become invisible. She believed it was time to give up on her dreams and focus on her grandchildren. She thought she had to trade in the little black dress for a muumuu. Even worse, you were now in danger of losing your husband to someone younger and sexier.

When it was Gladys' turn to experience "IT" she told herself there's no way I am going to follow in Mama's footsteps. She was willing and able to blaze her own trail. Gladys loves sex and she loves men and wasn't willing to give up either. After menopause Gladys was quick to notice she was still attracting lots of male attention. Sure her butt and her thighs might be less firm, and her stretch marks a little more noticeable but she was still willing and able to strut her stuff. With that attitude she was able to attract a younger guy who thinks she's fabulous and is always aiming to please her.

I met Gladys recently at one of my Real Cougar Lunch Parties. She is beautiful, vibrant and full of life. I can understand why younger men are attracted to her. The thing she says helps her sail through life is her sense of humor. She doesn't take herself too seriously and always appreciates a good laugh. I think adopting Gladys' attitude would be really beneficial for all of us Hormonal Hotties.

Chapter Six

"How old did you say you are?"

I'll bet you remember the jolt you felt the very first time someone called you "ma'am". To this day I cringe when I hear it directed at me. I want to say "hey are you talking to me"? All of us are very observant in noticing the people around us getting older, but we never want to believe it's happening to us. Thank goodness we are living in a world today where there's lots of help in erasing those uninvited reminders of time.

Let's be honest, what Real Cougar doesn't want to look 10 years younger? Who doesn't want someone to ask, "How old did you say you are?" because you look so good? None of us want to look 25, but don't you want to look sensational for the age you are right now? Yes, I know it's internal beauty that really counts but why not have the outer match the inner so you are a beautifully complete package?

Let's be honest, what Real Cougar doesn't want to look 10 years younger? There are a multitude of products and services that promise to make us look younger, but there are some basics that you need to follow. Nothing is more appealing than a Real Cougar with beautiful skin, subtle makeup a flattering haircut and knowing how to dress with fabulous flair.

Skincare

One of the best known ways to look youthful and vibrant is to take good care of your skin. You need to keep it hydrated, clean, protected from the sun, and free of discoloration. Those are the basics.

Margret Avery agrees. Margret is a New York City based make-up artist and beauty writer. For over 28 years she has been a noted skin care maven who is always searching for the next best thing. Margret has worked with award winning photographers like David Seidner, advised on shoots for Vanity Fair, Harper's Bazaar, Elle, The New York Times Magazine and Vogue. She has made the faces of Virginia Madsen, Annette Benning, Christy Turlington, Susan Sarandon and Cindy Crawford, even more beautiful. I am pleased this busy lady agreed to share some of her expert advice on how to look fabulous after forty.

Margret is constantly asked how she keeps her skin and the skin of her A-list clients looking so young and wrinkle free. She told me, "Keep it simple". After spending thousands of dollars on products and visits to many of New York's top dermatologists Margret wasn't getting the results she was looking for. So, being a Real Cougar she took matters into her own hands and custom designed an effective 4-part skincare regime. It's really easy to follow, it works beautifully and has the added bonus of being gentle on your pocketbook.

Margret's Magic Formula:

1. At night treat your skin gently using only a facial oil or cleansing cream to take off makeup. Important to note – don't use water.
2. Use a toner that is either salicylic acid based or just plain rosewater to prevent breakouts and remove last traces of makeup.
3. Finish by applying a firming serum or night cream.
4. In the morning cleanse your skin with a warm, damp washcloth and a gel cleanser, if needed. The washcloth aids in gentle exfoliation. Then apply your day serum.

Margret was amazed to see how much better her skin looked as soon as she stopped using water on her face at night. Don't forget as a pro she can really pinpoint the differences that you and I would overlook. For the first time in a long time her skin was smooth and soft and she wasn't breaking out anymore. Plus, her skin was feeling much more hydrated. Keeping our skin hydrated is one of the most important things we can do after 40. As we age it's the *hydration that keeps wrinkles from forming.*

When applying your moisturizer, favorite serum or cream make sure you don't forget to treat your neck and your decolette. Too many women neglect the obvious and you can see the end result of that neglect very easily. You want the skin on your face, neck and chest to match. It all has to be uniformly smooth.

One last thing that's so easy to do and yet is often overlooked. *Exfoliate your skin.* Getting into the habit of doing it at least once a week will make dull aging skin glow! There's plenty of refinishing products on the market that warm the skin creating a more radient look. They provide an at-home alternative to microdermabrasion and they really do work well.

Makeup That Will Take 10 Years Off Your Face

Your skin is constantly changing and that's why you have to keep up-to-date with your makeup and how you apply it. The products that you used at 30 are not the same products you should be using at 40 and beyond.

But, before you throw away all your cosmetic products, do yourself the biggest favor and *make an appointment to see a really good makeup professional.* This doesn't mean going into your favorite department store and getting a free makeover. Remember these people are paid by the number of products they sell, that's not what you want. Makeup pros will spend the time teaching you about the different products because they aren't pressured to fill a selling quota. They will also share the best techniques for applying makeup properly. And, here's the best part - they will watch you do your own face to make sure you've got it right. It's imortant to find someone who really knows how to use color to accentuate the positive and hide your flaws - that's make such a huge difference. When applying makeup it's all about the technique. When done right it can take 10 years of your face instanteously.

I started to use Lauren Hutton's Face Disc after I heard her say this. "Most makeup available today is formulated for younger women. The textures are heavy, the colors saturated and they are filled with shiny particles that act like airport runway lights highlighting every line, wrinkle and pore."

Another thing that I like about the Face Disc is everything is in one compact. All my different colored concealers, blush, and eyebrow filler are all in one place and it's really great when I travel. Another bonus is that it comes with a video where Lauren shows you where and how to apply each product in the compact. I must say, when I use the Face Disc I see a dramatic improvement in how I look. It magically erases the ravages of time and stress.

Make-Up Tips From Margret

- keep your eye makeup more matte during the daytime, too much shimmer is aging
- wear a tinted moisturizer and concealer where needed

- always use 2 different shades of concealer, one for the facial area and one that is lighter for around the eyes and mouth
- a lighter concealer around the mouth before applying lipstick makes them more alluring
- curl your lashes, you want them to flirt for you
- keep your eyeliner soft, smudge the line, especially during the day time
- a cream blush always adds a bit of extra glow in a subtle way

Here's the bottom line on makeup after 40: Too much makes you look older.

Facelift or Injectable Filler?

If you are thinking about doing something about the sags, bags and wrinkles, you are probably wondering whether to get a facelift or try one of the less evasive cosmetic procedures. Today, more and more women are choosing the minimally invasive procedures which are referred to as "liquid face lifts." The more popular products being used for these procedures are Restylane, Juvederm Radiesse, Botox and Dysport.

The liquid lift uses injectable dermal fillers to plump up the skin from the inside out. They fill in wrinkles, restore facial fullness, and re-contour facial features to improve or enhance your look.

As minimally invasive procedures such as the liquid face lift become more and more popular, the debate grows about the advantages of these newer, less invasive treatments versus the traditional surgical approach. Every procedure regardless of how minor you may think it is warrants thoughtful consideration and research.

Advantages of the
Liquid Face Lift vs. a Traditional Face Lift

The most obvious advantage of the liquid rather than a traditional face lift is that improvements in the appearance of lines, wrinkles and sagging skin are similar and achieved without actual surgery. The use of injectables to plump up and fill out the face means that patients have a *much less invasive* option than was previously available to them. Although most people would probably cringe at the thought of getting needles stuck in their face, there is no actual cutting involved.

Because anesthesia is usually not required with most injectable procedures, the immediate risk to the patient is significantly less than with plastic surgery. Moreover, there is usually *no significant downtime required* following the procedure (although you may want to lay low for a day or two, unless you are prepared to answer questions about any redness or swelling that may occur at the injection sites).

Another advantage of a liquid face lift, in many cases, is a *more natural looking result* than is usually achieved with surgery. Because the skin is filled from the inside, there are no scars.

More importantly, though, the result is never a "pulled tight" or "windswept" look, as can occur with a traditional face lift. Many doctors believe that this method is much more akin to how nature makes us look young, because it deals with plumping or filling the skin instead of pulling it tight. This mimics the fullness we see in a youthful face.

Finally, liquid face lifts *cost much less* than traditional face lifts, and they can be *performed in all areas of the face*, including the forehead and around the eyes. In contrast, a traditional face lift deals only with the lower face, requiring a patient to get separate procedures to address the forehead and eye areas.

Disadvantages of the
Liquid Face Lift vs. a Traditional Face Lift

The downside to the use of dermal fillers is that, so far, their *track record is short.* As of now, there have been few reported serious complications, but those that have been reported include swelling, bruising, pain, itching, tenderness, visible bumps or lines under the skin, and allergic reactions. In addition, in very rare cases, a blood vessel can accidentally be punctured by a needle, potentially causing an embolism, necrosis (tissue death) or other significant damage to the skin.

Moreover, though the instances of the aforementioned complications are relatively rare, there is a bigger question for many people: What are the long-term effects, and when will we know? With technology that has been in use for such a relatively short period of time, there is frankly *no way to be certain about the possible long-term complications* or side effects.

The other check in the "con" column has to do with the longevity of the results. While a traditional face lift may get you 5, 10, or even 15 years of a more youthful appearance, most of the dermal fillers do *wear off* as the material is absorbed by the body. Therefore, the results of a liquid face lift may only last, on average, from six months to one year. This means more trips to your doctor and more injections. Over time, this also means that a liquid face lift can actually cost more than a traditional face lift, due to the cost of maintaining your results.

One more important note: Before choosing your doctor make sure you do your research. Ask your questions, and also insist on looking at their patient's before and after pictures. If you want a better look, ask for referrals. Make the effort to take these women out for a cup of coffee so you can see the results for yourself. Not all doctors are created equal so please do yourself a big favor and shop around.

The Mane Attraction

Since we were young girls our hair has been an ongoing obsession. It's seems no matter what kind of hair we have we are never satisfied. And, as we get older deciding on the perfect cut and color doesn't get any easier. In fact, after 40 we're expected to follow a whole new set of rules just so our hair is age appropriate, whatever that means.

You can drive yourself nuts deciding what is the best look for you. Should it be long, short, curly, straight, blond, highlights, bangs, no bangs and the list goes on. Here are a few tips that will help you figure out this complicated hair puzzle.

1. Heave-Ho to Small Hot Rollers

Are you still using small hot rollers? Then your hair probably looks out of date! The style today is wavy and loose and is best accomplished with extra large rollers or gently wrapping sections of your air around a curling iron. A 1940'S wave reminiscent of Veronica Lake is all the rage these days, so be sure you loosen up those locks.

2. Layer Your Hair

Want to keep your hair long, but don't want to look like you are desperately trying to hang onto your youth? Then try this simple trick. Layer your hair. Too many older women with long hair wear it stick straight like they did in high school. Follow the lead of celebs like Teri Hatcher, Cindy Crawford, Goldie Hawn, Jaclyn Smith and Renee Russo and add a little bounce with a good cut and a few layers to frame the face and create volume.

3. Color That Brightens

As we get older, we lose the natural luminosity of our skin. To kick it up a notch choose a hair color that brightens your face. Stay away from extremes, too blonde or too black doesn't work.

I would suggest going to a top-notch colorist for advice. Also, consider adding a few brightening highlights around your face. Lighter tones attract the eye. And, finally for you Real Cougars who have trouble keeping up with your gray roots, pick a high-lighting color that blends into the grey. That way those grays won't be as noticeable between touchups.

Your Signature Style

Your wardrobe and the way you put it together is so important. Just like the wrong makeup can make you look dated, so can wearing the wrong clothes. You have to put new benchmarks on what sexy looks like after 40. When I need help in that department I look to the experts at www.fabulousafter40.com, *JoJami Tyler and Deborah Bolan*. They are helping women over 40 find the right look at any age. They like to ask their clients this question, "Are you a half baked cookiethat looks pretty good, but with a few more minutes in the oven,you could be, oh so much more yummy?"

You have to put new benchmarks on what sexy looks like after 40. A Real Cougar knows that her wardrobe has to reflect both her age and her attitude. Gone are the days of the miniskirt and the backless dresses. Gone, too, are the skin-tight sweaters, halter tops and exposed navels.

I am not suggesting for one moment that you can't dress like the sexy Real Cougar that you are. What I am saying is you might have a closet full of clothes but nothing flattering to wear.

Here's a checklist you should put up in your closet to remind you what works and what doesn't.

7 Fabulous Ways To Take Off 10 Years in Ten Minutes

1. Break up a Matching Set

Still marrying your matching jackets to your matching pairs of pants? Then it's time for a divorce. This super coordinated look is old, dated and makes you look unoriginal (unless of course you are in a traditional work position that requires a formal business look).

For a casual dressing, weekends especially, try breaking up these two key pieces and pairing them with other things in your closet. So instead of brown jeans with a brown jean jacket, try brown jeans fun sweater wrap with or a brown jean jacket with t-shirt, flowy skirt and boots. Matching pieces may be easy but they are not hip. Put them with other items in your wardrobe and you'll project a more creative, playful you!

2. Lower your Neckline

An easy way to turn back the clock a few years is to open up your neckline. Real Cougars steer clear of tops and t-shirts that sit at the collarbone and opt for lower rounded necklines and v-necks. Another great option is to try a wrap top which will create the illusion of sexy. If you find that too low, just add a camisole to peek out at the V neck. A chunky necklace also helps to fill in the bareness.

3. Get Rid of the Glitter

Why is it some women make themselves up like a Christmas tree- even during the daytime? We're talking about those 40+ gals that go overboard with glitter and sparkle thinking shiny will make them look young. Whatever the reason, we encourage you to look a little closer. Too much flash can really age a gal. If you want to sparkle, do it with your jewelry, and keep the glitz on your garments to a minimum.

4. Pull Your Shirt Out

This one is easy. Just remember, chic women don't tuck in. Look around and you'll see what we mean. If you believe that an untucked top will look loose and messy then you are wearing the wrong top. Try a fitted t-shirt that follows the curves of your body shirt no matter what your size. A loose shirt pulled out on a size 4 or a size 24 will only make you look square and boxy.

5. Pass on Small Prints

Conjure up an image of a dowdy little old lady and you probably visualize a granny in a tiny flower print dress. Small prints (especially ones with little flowers) can look really matronly. And, if you have some meat on your bones, small prints will make you look heavier than you are. Got the picture?

6. Pass on Pearl and Gold Buttons

We know a lot of you are attached to your favorite old cardigans with the pearl buttons and shiny gold buttons, but these look old fashioned and too conservative for a Real Cougar. Instead opt for sweaters with modern plain flat buttons. And don't forget you can always replace buttons too. A beautiful button on a plain sweater can create a knock-out look.

7. Get Sexy with Shoes

Real Cougars know mini skirts and super low cut tops will make you look trashy, not classy after 40, but shoes are a fabulous way to still look sexy! Let your personality shine through with shoes that subtlety seduce or are a little more flirty and showy. Try dressing from the shoes up. Find a pair of shoes that really speak your style. Fall in love and buy them! Then find the outfit to work with the shoes. Never have your shoe compete with your outfit. A colorful patterned shoe goes best with solid neutral outfits. If you're trying an animal print shoe, don't overdo a good thing—one animal print per outfit. What's the very best thing about shoes? You may be having a bad day in the dressing room, but if you head on over to the shoe department, you'll always find a pair you fall in love with.

I know this is a lot of information to absorb but there's one last thing that's so very important to remember.

Staying beautiful, vibrant and youthful can be fun if you treat it that way. It's all about attitude. It's about stepping out of your comfort zone and trying something new and exciting. You may think looking fabulous is just superficial fluff, but it's not. When you start turning heads as you walk by or find yourself smiling when you look into the mirror, it is going to give your sagging confidence a real honest to goodness lift. That's a feeling you owe yourself at any age.

Chapter Seven

Sex is not a job

Here's another stupid myth that drives me crazy. Women over 40 have to pack up their sexuality and toss it into the back of the closet. Since when does sex come with an expiration date? In my opinion, sex just keeps getting better as you keep doing it. Don't they say, "practice make perfect"? So please don't even think of giving up something that is so much fun.

If you are finding sex ain't what it used to be you could be the victim of your own thoughts. If you don't think you are desirable you yourself are turning off the electricity. Sex becomes merely a mechanical act done out of a warped sense of duty. And, when sex stops being fun it just stops!

Women over 40 never have to pack up their sexuality and toss it into the back of the closet.

Sex is such a natural part of who we are. It's meant to be treasured as a truly beautiful part of the human experience. It's not something to be ashamed of and it certainly doesn't deserve to be discarded at 50, 60 or even 80. ***It's truly a gift that can keep on coming.***

I was lucky enough to have an enlightening conversation with Susan Quilliam, a sexologist and the author of the updated version of the classic book *The Joy of Sex*. Susan offers advice on this website www.susanquilliam.com and has written 18 books on love, sex and relationships. I guess that makes her a sexpert.

She says, "In the 36 years since the original Joy of Sex was published, presuppositions have shifted completely. Now we know about hormones, pheromones, and the importance of the clitoris. Now we have internet sex, and the Venus Butterfly. The original book was groundbreaking—but even cultural icons occasionally need a makeover."

Susan believes that both men and women have never been under more pressure to achieve in the bedroom: - to have good sex, to have more sex, to have better sex than the Joneses - despite the fact that the Joneses themselves, due to all the pressure, probably aren't having sex at all.

One of the ways we have gone wrong, according to Susan is we haven't recognized the emotional power of sex. "It's isn't a game—it's a subject we have to take seriously," she says.

Both men and women have never been under more pressure to achieve in the bedroom.

"When The Joy of Sex was first written, it was believed that sex and love could be separate. But most of us require a connection before we can do any more than simply perform; love may not be all you need, but it's essential for more than the most basic satisfaction. Equally, when the going gets rough in relationships, good, pleasurable sex can bring you through. ***When you make love, you do exactly that.***"

All right, if what Susan says is true, what do you do when sex loses its punch or is no longer an enjoyable part of your relationship? Do you leave, stay or resort to finding a friend with benefits?

Friends with Benefits

For those of you who may not be familiar with this term a friend with benefits or "benie" is a mutual practical arrangement for satisfying each other's sexual needs without the usual expectations of love, romance, or in most cases, monogamy. The thing about these arrangements is they don't always have equal benefits for both parties involved.

Not all, but most women likely will confuse sex with love, even when they say they just want sex. ***Whether you admit it or not, if you are a women you will get sucked into an emotional attachment.*** It's hard for any of us Real Cougars to keep our hearts under wraps when we are putting ourselves in such a vulnerable position (pardon the pun). Even the hard-hearted-hannahs do get their hearts broken.

It all boils down to asking yourself these two questions:

> 1. Am I strong enough to suffer the emotional ups and down of this non-commited relationship?

2. Is this FWB relationship okay because it's fun and just a rest stop on the way to a something more fulfilling.

Think about it and even if the answer is yes to both questions, are you sure you are ready to dive in?

I suppose the success of these relationships depends completely on the two people involved and the ground rules they establish. For some it may be just what the doctor ordered, while for others just another bump on an already hazardous emotional roller-coaster ride.

Dr. Pepper Schwartz, a Professor of Sociology at the University of Washington in Seattle and a relationship expert, fessed up about her relationships on Oprah. "At 62, I am having the best sex of my life. I am divorced after being married for over 20 years and am now exploring and expanding my sexual universe. During a lull in my dating schedule, I call upon my 'friend with benefits' to fill the void."

Here's Susan Quilliam's take on the subject of FWB's. "If sexual love can be — and it is — the supreme human experience, it must be also a bit hazardous. It can give us our best and our worst moments. Love involves someone else's neck besides your own. It's important to make sure you don't exploit or injure someone else." In other words make sure both of you are emotional equals there for the same reasons.

Loss of Sexual Desire

According to surveys more than a quarter of all baby boomers have stopped having sex altogether. That's a pretty shocking number don't you think? So, why does that happen? For women, it could be any number of reasons: loss of hormones, inability to achieve orgasm, too much emotional baggage or believing you are no longer sexy and desirable. Check out every possibility because many times there is more than one reason for your loss of interest.

David Schnarch, a clinical psychologist and certified sex therapist believes that couples are emotionally alienated from each other. People only have sex up to the level of their sexual development. *Foreplay isn't about sexual arousal, it's a negotiation for the level of intimacy and eroticism that will follow.*

According to surveys more than a quarter of all baby boomers have stopped having sex altogether.

When you are emotionally alienated from each other sex becomes boring. Schnarch says, "When two people get together, they have a negotiation. You get to decide what you don't want to do, I get what to decide what I don't want to do, and we do whatever is left. Normal sexual relationships consist of leftovers. No wonder we get bored. It stopped being fun."

Modern marriage is based on the idea of intimacy and partnership. If you go back 200 years, people never got married for intimacy. They were looking for a financial arrangement and/or political alliances. The intimacy we are searching so hard for today is something we never had. But our perception of the lack of it causes so many problems, including divorce.

Getting Back "The Tingle"

Now, for the bright side: Most of us are better in bed now in our 40's, 50's and 60's than we were in our 20's. We can learn intercourse in our teens, but learning to have an intimate sex life comes much later in our lives.

"The sex that you're looking for is hiding right under your nose," says Schnarch. "It's in the kissing. It's your mouth... *people can fake orgasms, but you can't fake connection and when you feel your partner really is not there on the other side of a kiss, you're usually not interested in going further.* Feeling your partner's intent is terribly important in sex. Most people focus on technique, but technique is sex without intent".

Keep your eyes open. Love is never blind. Sex with eyes closed and lights off is lonely and anonymous. *Seventy percent of people have sex with their eyes closed, while only 15% can have an orgasm with eyes open.* What does this mean? It means tuning out your partner. Don't do it.

Quilliam says, "Have sex whether or not you feel like it. The more you do it the more you will want to do it. Don't have sex unwillingly but fool around for 15 minutes – just to keep in practice." As women we get too involved with mothering and less involved with being a seductress. Go pull off your apron

and get into your sexy black nightgown and plan an adventur-
ous weekend away from the house.

Masturbation is another way of getting back the "the tingle".
Maybe it's just me, but I am still shocked every time I hear
a woman say she doesn't understand why she can't achieve
orgasm through intercourse. Why don't all women know that
clitoral stimulation is the way the majority of us become orgas-
mic? Orgasm is our reward for good sex and if you are not
getting that release you are cheating yourself.

If you are having trouble achieving orgasm try the do-it-your-
self method. Masturbation can be very enlightening. Touch
yourself, explore your body until you experience what makes
you hot and juicy. When you know where to touch yourself
you can teach any man how to do it. Masturbation doesn't have
to be done solo. Men love to watch you and learn from you as
you give yourself pleasure. Behind closed doors just let your
imagination run wild.

When I was in my middle twenties I was *Ogasm is our*
having sex but never had experienced an *reward for*
orgasm. I didn't miss it because I didn't know *good sex.*
what it was supposed to feel like. I enjoyed sex but I didn't
understand what all the shouting was about. So I decided to find
out.

I went out and bought a book that explained a woman's body
in vivid detail and it had great pictures so you could clearly see
what's what. I remember sitting in a big chair with the book

in one hand while the other hand started to explore my body. It didn't take very long to feel "the tingle" and the gradual buildup of excitement that climaxed in my climax. The experience left me breathless. Now I knew what all the shouting was about because I was shouting too! I loved it. After that, if a man wasn't 100% sure of where to touch me, I didn't have any problem teaching him how to make me smile.

Masturbation doesn't have to be done solo.

The One-Hour Orgasm

Many Real Cougars are heading back to school, learning how to achieve sex that is off the charts. They are learning not to rush the act and be fully immersed in the experience. That's why Tantric Sex and the one-hour orgasm otherwise known as the EMO, or extended massive orgasm are regaining popularity.

What exactly is the one-hour orgasm? From what I gather it's all about the contractions. During what most people consider a normal orgasm, men generally have 6 to 9 contractions each lasting for about 8/10ths of a second. For women it's about 9 to 12 each lasting the same 8/10th of a second.

At The Institute for Human Abilities in California, they teach "Basic Sensuality 101" which includes a how-to instructional for the "Venus Butterfly" technique. If you can achieve the one hour orgasm you graduate with honors. At the Institute they call the typical 6 - 12 contraction orgasm a "genital sneeze". Not that the sneeze is bad, but we could all be doing a whole lot better.

Drs. Steve and Vera Bodansky give courses on how to have a better sex life. They have been publicly giving demonstrations of what is potentially possible in the realm of orgasms since 1980. They live on the west coast but twice a year they travel east to demonstrate their techniques at the School of Womanly Arts in New York City. If you're not brave enough to enroll in the course, maybe you want to read their latest book, The Illustrated Guide to Extended Massive Orgasm.

It's never too late to learn new things. Sex is not a contest, it's supposed to be fun. You are not being judged on beauty and talent so stop being so critical of yourself. How can you possibly enjoy sex if you're preoccupied with holding in your stomach or focused on your jiggly thighs? Believe me when I tell you that the men are not half as tough on you as you are on yourself. They tell me they are just happy to have a warm, responsive, woman in bed with them. There should only be one thing on your mind when you're having sex and that's making each other happy.

One more thing:

How can you possibly enjoy sex if you're preoccupied with holding in your stomach or focused on your jiggly thighs?

Be safe not sorry. Safe sex is a must. If you are venturing out into the world of dating, you must insist that any man you have relations with wear a condom. Too many unsuspecting women are contracting sexually transmitted diseases (STD's) and they are no fun. Nothing is more important than protecting yourself. I won't dwell on this because I know you know what I am talking about.

So, Real Cougars now there's only one thing left to do. Go get 'em. Laugh about sex, have fun with sex, explore new ways to enjoy sex. Sex is not a job—it's a wonderful, knock your socks off gift just waiting to be unwrapped.

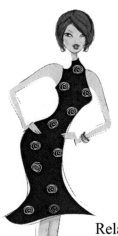

Chapter Eight
You Don't Complete me

Relationships are always tough. ***Putting two people together and expecting them to become one unit creates all sort of problems.*** Yet, for better or for worse, the majority of you want to be part of this socially accepted union known as a "couple". Successfully navigating through all the potential landmines of that partnership takes a truckload of patience and stamina. A touch of insanity doesn't hurt either!

All of us, no exceptions, walk into a relationship with baggage. Those unresolved wounds on our psyche we've been talking about throughout the book. It's tough taking responsibility for your own happiness. That's why consciously or unconsciously you are all looking for the person with the power to do it for you. Of course, deep in your gut you know that's not possible, but you keep searching just the same.

All of us, no exceptions, walk into a relationship with baggage.

Then one day you find him – Mr. Right. Your hormones start to rage and you believe you have found the answer to your prayers. He feels the same way about you and so you make the decision to create a new life together. In the beginning life is grand, and you are walking around on Cloud Nine. Then one day, out of the blue, something he does, says or implies opens up a an old would and the hurts come oozing out.

Your Mr. Right has fallen down on the job. He's not making you happy – he's not the guy you thought he was. So how do you show your hurt and disappointment? You punish him. You may do it in ways that are passive aggressive, but believe me he's getting the message. You have changed dramatically and he wonders why. *Your resentment, matched with his disappointment and confusion, are the beginning of the downward spiral.* It's not surprising that the divorce rate in this country is 50% and rising.

I painted an all-too-familiar picture, because every Real Cougar has to ask herself this question: *What can I do to avoid falling into that all too familiar relationship trap ever again?*

The answer is obvious. You must go where you have always been afraid to go ---deep inside yourself. There are no shortcuts when it comes to a good relationship. It takes understanding, it takes constant attention, it needs two people who are willing to accept each other warts and all. It takes you being authentic.

My 3 Top Real Cougar Relationship Tips:

1. Be the partner you want your partner to be. Don't expect to attract your Mr. Right if you don't possess the same qualities you are looking for in him.

2. Take ownership of what isn't working in your relationship. Stop pointing the finger of blame at someone else.

3. Create a relationship vision together. Find someone who wants the same things you do. Opposites might attract but they very rarely last for the long haul.

Start doing the work necessary to heal your own wounds. Don't look for anybody else to do that for you – it can't be done. When you feel complete, you're not looking for someone else to complete you. Be okay with who you are and you will attract the right person for the right reasons.

Be okay with who you are and you will attract the right person for the right reasons.

Here are some stories of Real Cougars just like you who understand the importance of "I CREATE". They did the work necessary to really get what they want out of life. These women are the magnets that attracted men who are loving, secure and commited to their nurturing relationship. I hope they will inspire you as they have inspired me.

Beth's Story

Beth is 48 and a member of my Real Cougar Woman Club. Her story proves it's never too late for change. Beth married young and had a child, but as the years passed discovered that she wanted much more from her marriage. She was evolving, discovering new ways to get excited about life but her husband was stuck in the "what-is". Her decision to leave was not done in haste. She was married for 18 years before Beth decided to divorce. That might seem like an awfully long time but it was a gut wrenching decision. Her husband was a good man and a good father – but he wasn't good for her. After the divorce she said, "I never want to marry again, and as much as I love my son, I wouldn't even consider having any more kids."

Then she met Rick. She wasn't looking for another man. In fact, she was happy not to be in involved with anyone. Beth was learning to be on her own and in the process becoming a strong independent woman. But here he was, this 27 year old man who thought she was the best thing since sliced bread. He made her feel loved and made her feel vibrant and sexy. That kind of attention would be hard for any of us to resist. Beth was cautious at first, but Rick's persistence paid off and she found herself becoming more relaxed and more invested in making this new relationship work.

It was clear from the beginning that Rick was serious about his commitment. So serious in fact that he asked Beth to move in with him. Beth was excited by the offer but she was also afraid. She knew in order to make such a big decision she would have to be totally up front about all her concerns. She had evolved into a Real Cougar who knew what she wanted and he had to know that going in. She wanted to be 100% truthful about retaining her independence in every way including financial. Beth also made it clear about not wanting marriage and more children. She followed her heart, but at the same time, left no stone unturned.

Beth and Rick have been living together for 2 years now. She feels, loved, respected and safe. I remember her calling to tell me that she might even have had a slight change of heart about remarrying. Of course, as soon as she felt the shift in her attitude she let Rick know immediately. Beth says, "I really like having him in my life. Because I was a Real Cougar going into this relationship, everything he brings to the table is just icing on an already delicious cake."

Carole's Story

Like Beth, Carole Brody Fleet found herself alone, but not by choice. Her husband died after a long illness. After that chapter of her life ended Carole, then 40, wondered if she would ever find love again – or if she even wanted to.

Carole, author of Widows Wear Stilettos, says, "If it is difficult to go out alone as a woman, it is twice as difficult if you are a 'People Person', who is used to and in fact, in love with being surrounded by a crowd." Yet she knew that the only way that she could truly move forward and eventually open up her heart to another male presence in her life for all of the right reasons, was to make absolutely sure that she could go out and enjoy herself...all by herself.

For most women that is a pretty terrifying thought. Going out to dinner, to a museum or taking a vacation solo means you really have to take a giant leap out of your comfort zone. Carole started venturing out on her own in small ways - lunch at a coffee shop with a newspaper; coffee at a coffeehouse with a book. When she felt stronger and more confident she "graduated" to going to movies and comedy clubs by herself minus the books or newspapers. Later still, she started going to concerts, plays and fine dining establishments at night by herself - and guess what? She didn't turn into a pumpkin!

Her biggest "challenge" that she issued to herself came almost two years after her husband Mike's death. Following a business conference in Las Vegas she stayed on for one extra day. She dined, gambled, meandered through shops and enjoyed her favorite city all by herself. Of the experience, Carole said that, "It felt rather like the first day of kindergarten - except with champagne and slot machines."

When she returned home, she then knew that she could genuinely enjoy herself, without a man or her daughter, or any kind of "distraction". And when the time came to introduce someone into her life, it would be because she was legitimately ready for a companion; not because of a glaring void that needed to be filled.

You can visit Carole at www.widowswearstilettos.com

Robyn Carey Allgever

One Saturday morning in February I spent two hours on the phone with Robyn. We had never spoken before but we immediately bonded. That's what happens in the Real Cougar community. I asked Robyn to share her story for this book and she was more than willing to do so.

In 1994, at the age of 39, Robyn began writing the first terrifying new chapter of her life – that of a single working mother of 3 children ages 4, 6 and 11. The one saving grace at the time was choosing to move home to Cincinnati, where her mother, step-father and a brother still resided and where she once had enjoyed a career in arts administration. Within three months Robyn landed her old job back as PR director at the Cincinnati Opera. Daycare in place, kids enrolled in school, she was off to a great start as a new single person.

Robyn, wasn't particularly afraid of dating. She tried the newspaper personals once – remember those days? "SDF seeking blah, blah, blah!" She tried long-distance dating for about a year with a successful business owner from Michigan. Very romantic, he would drive down and back in a day just to see her for a couple of hours. Too bad he didn't tell Robyn, he wasn't divorced, only separated! She had tucked away fourteen years worth of lack of trust issues, and this bit of news basically broke the bank for her.

She dated a classical pianist whose depression got the better of him...and us. Then a younger man living the life of a bohemian paid for by his trust fund. For all his eccentricities, and he had many, he did help Robyn to realize she was living her life as a victim. Until then she had worn it like armor – protecting her from the world. However, he wanted more of her and less of the children, so again...so long, farewell!

Robyn had a number of single friends by then, and they all had different priorities depending on the pressure of their jobs, children and emotional health. She admired one of my friends who approached finding men like a job search. That was not her style. However, she longed for a relationship and as time passed her anxiety increased. She felt angry, hopeless at times and even helpless. One summer afternoon while at the pool with a friend, who was recounting the details of the latest dating service she had discovered, Robyn had an epiphany!

She knew she was over it. She wasn't going to look for, worry about or waste another minute wondering about a relationship. It was crystal clear - she was missing so many wonderful aspects of life and her children's lives while desperately trying to control something that was out of her control! As soon as she realized that she makes her own happiness, the fear evaporated and she felt truly thrilled to be alive and even to be alone.

Three months later Rob, a friend Robyn had made several years before, reconnected and fell in love.

They have now been married for 7 years. He is nearly 18 years her junior. He was born in the fall of my senior year of high school! A jazz pianist, he is an old soul—he was listening to

Count Basie and Frank Sinatra on his grandfather's record player, while his peers were blasting Bon Jovi on their Walkman's. His family wasn't even fazed when he announced, "I am dating a 44-year old divorced woman with three children!" (By the way, Robyn's in-laws are only 4 years older than she is!)

Rob had never been married before and now he was the stepfather to my 3 children. That's not easy. The kids had known him for nearly four years before they were married, however moving in and dealing with the day-to-day challenges is very different. The kids were 19, 13 and 12 on their wedding day. Her son had just graduated from HS and went off to college, but the girls were just entering those fun teenage years! In order to meet these challenges, Robyn and Rob were pro-active and sought family counseling. Robyn says, "Don't kid yourself! If you don't know how to fix it...go to an expert!

Robyn believes any good relationship is all about communication. Don't wait and hope he figures it out. Because if he doesn't, you have to deal with the disappointment and even anger, while he remains baffled and hurt. Being direct comes much more naturally to Rob, and Robyn is eternally grateful for what he has taught her.

Robyn wanted to make sure I conveyed this important message.

"To my fellow Cougars, I say, don't worry about the age difference. It never bothered Rob – he was the one who initiated turning our friendship into a romance. Our relationship works, because we have tremendous respect for ourselves and for each other. Any healthy relationship has to start there. We also live by the motto, "if it isn't fun, it isn't worth doing!"

I want to thank these wonderful women who so generously shared their lives with us on these pages. Their stories illustrate that in order to *be happy you first have to be comfortable walking in your own shoes.* Only then will you find the right person to walk along side you. That's what makes Real Cougars so special. We are willing to do whatever it takes in the pursuit of happiness.

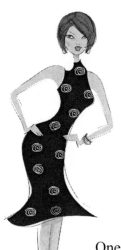

Chapter Nine

Creating Your Own Love Story

One cold January morning, which happened to be her 40th birthday, Ronnie Ann Ryan woke up to the realization she might be single for the rest of her life. Overall, she loved her life—she had plenty of friends, a great business, but Ronnie wanted something more. She desired a loving relationship and was disappointed that this never had materialized in her life. Even though she didn't "need" a man, she came to the conclusion she wanted to find the right one for her.

Within a few months Ronnie got serious about changing her single status. Summoning up all her determination, she vowed to do everything possible to change her relationship status. She set out to understand what had kept her single so she could now change those things. She realized she hadn't been open to men since her college sweetheart had broken her heart 18 years earlier!

To remedy this situation, Ronnie worked to open her heart to love and improve her self-image. She told everyone what she was up to and before she knew it, went out on her first blind date. That started her journey - Ronnie dated 30 men in 15 months before finally meeting her husband, Paul (number 30). They've been happily married for several years.

To get the results you want - do something different. This is what Ronnie tells all the women who enroll in her dating and relationship seminars. Here are her top tips and I love them.

7 Ways to Find Your Great Guy:

1. Smile and Be Friendly

This may sound too obvious but it's a great piece of dating advice. You'd be surprised how many people have forgotten basic social skills like smiling and saying hello. In your busy day, you may find yourself very focused on the tasks at hand and as a result, don't look up much from what you are doing. This could be true at your desk, on the train or in the grocery store. But there are opportunities to meet new people all the time once you lift up your head, look around you and start interacting with others.

When you notice someone giving you the eye, what is your immediate reaction? Do you think, "Oh no, he's looking at me!" and turn away quickly? Or do you smile first before turning your head gracefully? Noticing your reaction is the first step to greater awareness of how you relate to men. If you do return the smile that's great! Dating is a numbers game. So go ahead and grace a few men with your pearly whites to improve your odds for finding love.

2. Build Your Self-Confidence and Self-Image

Dating involves rejection – it's a piece of the puzzle that cannot be avoided. In order to survive the snubs you may encounter, you need to feel confident and have a good self-image. Over 80% of your beauty depends on how you feel about yourself inside.

Ultimately, you want to shore up your self-image so if and when you do face rejection, you won't be crushed. Positive self-talk can turn around the worst situation so be sure to use it generously.

3. Get Out to Meet New People

The chances of Prince Charming knocking on your door are between slim and none. If you want to find a mate, you have to get out there! Many women tell me they are tired after work or don't have time because there is too much to do. Well, if you don't have time to look for men, how will you have time for a man in your life? You need to clear space in your busy schedule to mingle with singles.

Once you decide to make time for dating, there are plenty of places to go. The place to find single men is at singles related events. Many women resist going to single events,

If you don't have time to look for men, how will you have time for a man in your life?

but that's where the single men are. Consider these singles options to maximize your search efforts: Dances. Speed Dating, Singles Groups (like Parent without Partners and Meetup.com), Singles Events at museums or sports arenas, online dating, and matchmakers.

Please don't rule out blind dates. Sometimes your friends and colleagues actually do come up with a great guy for you to meet.

Another tip – visit your local Home Depot or Hardware Store. Men love that stuff. You are not going to find the man of your dreams shopping for women's shoes or in your favorite spa.

4. Don't Forget to Flirt

Your feminine charm is your true power as a woman. It's our given right to flirt, but let's define what flirting really is. It's a non aggressive way of conveying that you are available and approachable. It can be done by using eye contact, smiling and friendly. It is definitely not being overtly vampish or sexually aggressive.

We've come a long way baby since the 60's and 70's with the sexual revolution and women's liberation. We can make it in a man's world, enjoy being financially independent and equal to men in many ways. That's all great for the work place. Unfortunately, these traditionally masculine skills are not useful in your romantic life. In fact, men may react to you competitively should you apply those busi-

Traditionally masculine skills are not useful in your romantic life.

ness skills in the dating arena. You don't want to invoke competition because there's nothing romantic about a man competing with you.

5. Resist Your Urge to Pursue

This is the single most crucial strategy of all to improve your dating success. As a "Chick in Charge" you know how to get things done and make things happen. However as I mentioned earlier, your business skills aren't useful when looking for love. Dating is still an archaic mating ritual that still requires "The Chase".

Surprisingly, in this day and age, it's still the man's job to pursue you. You may want to get the ball rolling with a certain man, but usually it won't work. Men prefer to pursue. While some guys who say they like aggressive women who ask them out, in the end, the vast majority still want to be in charge.

Think of dating like ballroom dancing. Dancing depends on having one leader and one follower. Two leaders cause toes to be stepped on and two followers won't allow you to go any where. To imitate "Dancing with the Stars", you'll need to let the man lead.

The chase gets a man invested in winning you over. If you make it too easy and serve yourself up on a silver platter, he'll probably lose interest.

Think of dating like ballroom dancing.

Men understand how to pursue. It's part of their DNA – to be the hunter. Don't fight nature because you think your fellow might be a "shy guy" who needs a little poke to get things going. Not true. You don't want a man who needs you to lead unless you want to lead ALL THE TIME. That gets tiring for even the most independent woman who probably prefers to be with a confident man who can share the leadership burden.

6. Independence is Great, But Don't Hit Him Over the Head with It

I know you can do everything without a man. You don't need a man for the paycheck, the financial stability, or even to have a baby. Today, having a relationship with a man is a choice. So, if you want that choice, you have to play the game. Not a game of manipulation and dishonesty, but one with rules that cannot be denied if you want success.

To be in a relationship with a man means you have to make room for him to be "the man." How you talk about your life and your independent nature can be a huge turn off.

The very nature of being in a relationship requires compromise and sacrifice to some extent. How many times have your heard a woman say "I won't settle?" That's fine, don't settle. But make that decision consciously. Somehow in our quest for independence women have forgotten that being in a relationship is about being interdependent. That's one of the benefits of partnership in business or love – having someone to rely on and share the burden.

Men and women may be more equal than ever, but please don't make the disastrous mistake of believing you are the same.

7. Date with Your Head, Not Just Your Heart

Dating is an emotional enterprise. It's about finding love which can be glorious or, at times, heart-wrenching. You can't date and avoid being vulnerable because your heart won't be open. Without an open heart, you can't connect at the heart level.

Men and women may be more equal than ever, but please don't make the disastrous mistake of believing you are the same. Using your head combined with your heart is vitally important to help navigate your way through these emotional waters. There are instances when you cannot simply trust your feelings and what your heart tells you. How many savvy business women do you know who throw all their street smarts out the window for love? Don't let this happen to you – it's the surest road to heart break hill. That's why it's advisable to date with your head, and not just your heart.

If you are prone to picking men with similar flaws, make a Red Flag List of the behaviors you want to avoid in the future. When you pay attention to these red flags, you minimize the risk of repeating the same mistakes.

Branch out. Try something different. Push yourself to be open to qualities other than a charming guy who sweeps you off your feet. Use your head and not just your heart to make smarter decisions and find the healthy, loving relationship you want and deserve.

Real Cougar Dating Successes

Lillie's Story

Lillie was a very successful sales person with many awards, plenty of friends and a close-knit family. Still, her desire for love was undeniable. She'd been attending traditional singles events but as luck would have it, Lillie met Bart through work — he was a potential client. She had called Bart several times trying to schedule a meeting. They played phone tag for weeks leaving each other business messages with a slightly flirtatious edge.

One day Lillie decided to take a chance and turn up the heat with Bart. She didn't know if this would get her the meeting, but she made a spontaneous decision to go for it. In her next voicemail she said she was happy to keep trading messages because she enjoyed listening to his sexy voice. Bingo—that got his attention! Bart returned her call quickly to set up the appointment to meet.

Turns out Lillie did land the account and Bart too. She couldn't help being attracted to this younger man who pursued her like no one had in a long time. Lillie was worried about their age difference, but Bart didn't even ask how old she was. Eventually he saw her driver's license and told her to stop worrying.

They've been together for four years and their relationship is going strong.

Gail's Story

Gail was a very practical woman who had built a solid computer hardware business, and enjoyed volunteering and spending time with friends and family. She was comfortable with things and had taken to dressing down, wearing jeans because she was always lugging boxes around. Over time she stopped wearing makeup because it just took up too much of her time.

Then Gail made a decision. For one week she'd try wearing her skirts again to see if anything would change. She also vowed to put on a touch of makeup and try being friendlier to people.

Turned out her efforts were well-rewarded. In as little as one week, people responded very differently to her. Men started noticing her. Several struck up conversations out of the blue. Even women seemed nicer and more helpful. Gail decided to extend her experiment into the future and that was the beginning of an incredible transformation.

Within a few months, Gail met a man at a trade show who she started to see. It wasn't long before the two were an item and Gail was smiling from ear to ear. Imagine, it all started with a simple wardrobe change and an intention to be more feminine and friendly.

Was it the skirt and lip balm or the way she felt about herself that attracted more attention for Gail? I think the change in her self-image and intention created the shift.

"The possibility of finding love over 40 is better than ever", says Ronnie Ann Ryan. "With half of the U.S. adult population being single, you're chances are excellent for finding the man of your dreams". She found love at 41, with a wonderful man four years her junior. Nobody thought Ronnie would ever marry and neither did she. That is why she re-evaluated her part in why she was single. That's how she knows and I know too, you can do exactly the same thing. Just be smart about your search methods, smile and be friendly, date with your head and not just your heart and it will happen.

People fall in love every day. Why not you?

I want to thank Ronnie Ann Ryan for helping me with this chapter. Since I only write about what I have experienced myself I didn't have an up-to-date perspective about dating. Sure I hear stories all the time, but that's not the same as being out in the trenches yourself. That's why I sought out a pro with a great track record.

For more information on Ronnie Ann Ryan's books and coaching please visit her website http://www.nevertoolate.biz.

Chapter Ten
Doing What You Love
-and Making Money Too

Using the skills we've developed throughout our careers, many of us Real Cougars are recreating ourselves as entrepreneurs. We are looking to call the shots and take control of our financial futures. According to the Bureau of Labor Statistics baby boomers account for over 56% of the self employed.

Of course, starting a business is not for the faint of heart. It means long hours, substantial start-up costs and learning a myriad of new skills. I know when I was in corporate I had lots of people there to help me. Now the buck stops at my desk. It's up to me to find the help, pay for the help and figure out the business strategy that will make my business profitable.

Starting a business is not for the feint of heart. Talk to any coach and they will tell you the key to making any new business a success is doing what you love to do, and finding a need that is screaming to be filled.

Five Questions You Have To Ask Yourself

1. What do I do best?

2. What information do other people come to me for?

3. What have I always dreamed of doing?

4. How will achieving my dream affect other people?

5. Will I always have regrets if I don't give it a try?

Through trial and lots of error, women today are taking the business world by storm. According to Womenentrepreneur.com, women-owned firms are the fastest growing in the country. I am always inspired when I hear stories of women who with a single idea went on to create an empire. Sarah Blakely, the creator of Spanx, is a great example of that. Imagine starting a business with just a pair of panty hose that you felt would serve a better purpose with no feet.

Not only are women entrepreneurs doing well, women in corporate jobs are making giant strides as too. In March 2009 a record of thirty women were appointed to Corporate Boards. Major companies like Microsoft, Pepsi, and Revlon are starting to appreciate the depth of experience of women in the workforce.

All of us have a unique opportunity in these 'tough economic times' to finally bring women into parity with our male counterparts. Elizabeth Gilbert, founder of Flourishing Business and author of The Chic Entrepreneur says, "Whenever you hear someone bemoaning the economy, say to yourself – "I am glad that I am in business right now". This is no time to fuss and worry or to be held back by lingering insecurities, you are a Real Cougar and this is the time to take charge and build your dream business. This is the perfect time to position yourself as a serious player.

Elizabeth says, "turn times of trouble into times of triumph and take your business career to the next level".

Elizabeth's Five Tips For Achieving Success

1. Throw out the old male model and lead with a hybrid approach. Repressing your sexuality in the workplace is no longer necessary. Today there is a new opening for blending the male and the female styles of work for more balance and fulfillment. Traditional business was built in a very male paradigm – more is better, control, domination, military style leadership. This culture created long workdays, long meetings, stress, and an over emphasis on short-term gains with a failure to take into account the long-term ramifications. *Now it's clear that the masculine needs to be balanced with the feminine*. Now it's time for the women to take charge too. With all of your past success behind you, you are well positioned to rise up and shine. Don't hold back your power.

2. Convey trust, the old fashioned way and the high tech way. Another emotional fallout of an economic crisis is that people's trust is rocked, so for new customers that don't already know you, you want to give them the assurance they need to trust you - that's half of what they are buying. Whether it's a firm handshake while looking someone right in the eyes, a genuine smile, sending a personal note in the mail, an extra follow up phone call, bonding, insurance, displaying the security of your website, or offering a money back satisfaction guarantee, these gestures are ways you and your staff can reduce a buyers' perceived risk level and show that you are trustworthy.

3. Get very clear on what you want. It is time to name and claim what you deserve. If you want a million dollar business, than build it. If you want to be in the C –suite, than put yourself there. And if you want to work only 20 hours a week or entirely virtually, then make it happen. *Start with a vision, turn the vision into a written plan, break that up into monthly and weekly goals and start checking them off.* It's easy to get sidetracked when we are not crystal clear on what we want, or to let the "shoulds" of others cloud our view. Write a letter to yourself committing to achieving your vision. Sign it, date it and keep it in your top desk drawer. Whenever you feel yourself getting sidetracked, remember what you have committed to and get yourself back on track by tackling the next to do in your plan.

4. Pick up the phone and work your network. We all know that it is a good business practice to "get out and network." Many times this game feels more like a business card collection scavenger hunt, than hanging out with girlfriends and laughing it up – but it doesn't have to. Networking when done right is just as fun as chatting with girlfriends. At this point you've made the rounds, you've met a lot of people, and you realized you are not going to be friends with everyone and that is OK. What matters is that you do find people that you do like, respect and admire. Now its time to grow those relationships and turn your contacts into true business allies. *People do business with those they like, know and trust* and what better way to remind them that they know, like and trust you, than to give them a ring? Have one or two specific things you want to ask them so the conversation feels structured and productive. People love to share their opinion. Then update them on what you've been up to and what you want. That's right—tell them what you want. Now that you are clear about it, it won't take you more than a sentence or 2 to describe. You'll sound focused and definitive, and you'll be amazed at how often they'll offer to do something to help you get it.

5. Work the Value Conscious mindset. Consumers all over the world are re-classifying themselves as value conscious. Supposedly it is now en vogue to scrimp, save and even look at price tags. An easy way to sell directly to customers' new self identity is to have an option that is specifically, for the Value Conscious. So whatever you are selling, add a way for people to save money get in at a lower price tier. Be prepared to demonstrate how much they'll save– whether it's a handbag or a hamburger. But don't make this your only offer. We are not throwing the high end, luxury choice away. First of all, you need your high end line to illustrate the value choice's afford-ability by comparison. Secondly, remember that not everyone has jumped on this bandwagon, and even the ones who have are still worth tempting. ***Ironically, it is usually the highest tier product in the bunch that offers the most real value.*** And it won't be long until value regains its true meaning, not cheap but getting the most for your money.

Another one of my Real Cougars recently shared her story with me. It touched me and so I now I want to share it with you. This is a great example of how you can succeed in business with nothing but a dream, a deep passion, and a never-give-up attitude.

Rennu's Story

As I look back at my life, the past 22 years has been quite a journey. November 21, 1991 – a day I will never forget. It was a bleak cold winter day, a week before Thanksgiving and I was expecting to meet my husband for lunch. As I waited for him it was hard for me to comprehend the change in my heart. Our relationship had only gotten worse since the birth of our second daughter. I was no longer in love with him but stayed for the sake of the kids. It's a bad reason to stay, but I felt stuck with no other options. My husband and I had very little to say to each other, and the worse part was I was aware he was having an affair with my secretary. I endured the daily insults and pain for the simple reason that divorce is not looked upon favorably in the Indian culture.

So on this day I waited and waited for him to appear but he never did. I knew in my heart something had to be wrong. I called the office several times and got no answer, so just decided to head home. When I arrived I got the most unbelievable shock. There he was coming down our driveway in a U-Haul truck loaded with all of our worldly possessions. He almost ran me over as he yelled out the window "you'll get your present later". At 7pm, the doorbell rang and I was served with divorce papers.

When I look back now, after all these years, I realize that my divorce was a blessing in disguise. Had I continued in that marriage I would not have lived my dreams and aspirations. He took what he considered were the most valuable things, the TV, couches, Armani suits, jewelry, and all the cash we had earned from our thriving franchises. He did however leave my most valuable possession behind – two beautiful daughters.

Raising my girls as a single working mom meant I was con-stantly looking for good day care. This was a struggle. I went from day care to preschools never quite satisfied with the results I was getting. Eventually I decided to work from home so I could spend time teaching them what they needed to know. It was at that point I knew in my heart that one day I would open a school. I would provide kids with exactly the right environment and curriculum to encourage learning.

Between 1991 and 2001 I put away every extra penny for my dream school. I opened the doors to my first learning center, Genius Kids, in 2001 with only two children. Today I feel I have achieved the American Dream as I manage and operate 5 award winning learning centers with over 200+ students. Now I am getting ready to launch the first early learning online preschool in the world.

My journey as a single mom has not been easy one. I have experienced bitter child custody battles, lost a home in foreclosure, endured debilitating attorney fees, and there were times I barely had $10.00 in my purse for gas. However, now I can say proudly that I have been successful at climbing the ladder of success.

Rennu has received much recognition for her work. She is the recent recipient of the 2009 " Outstanding 50 Asian Americans in Business Award".

To find out more about Rennu's school go to:
www.geniuskidsonline.com or missrennuonline.com

Your Business Image is Important

Whether you are a small business owner or a corporate executive, your overall business persona is your calling card. You have learned by now, that perception is 75% of the success equation. What people believe either makes things flow more smoothly or makes the ride a lot rougher. That's why it makes sense to always present the best image possible. First impressions open the door and allow you to sell your expertise.

Stephen Viscusi, the Founder and CEO of bulletproofyourresume.com and the author of "Bulletproof Your Job" offers helpful *Perception is 75% of the success equation.* hints on how to fit into today's workplace. This is especially important for those of you Real Cougars who are deciding to re-enter the world of business after a long absence.

Stephen says, "you need to learn the fine art of being perceived as younger and it's more than just the way you look." Is this fair? Is it even legal? Maybe not, but it's part of doing what's necessary to hold onto your job, get a new one, or boost the image of your own business.

For those who are unemployed, you must do whatever it takes to convey to hiring managers that you are employable. What does this mean? No one wants to hire someone who's stuck in the old-fashioned way of thinking, Being qualified, working hard and being loyal to a company is not enough any more. Your Princeton degree and enviable references won't get you as far as you think in today's job market.

Stephen says, "It's no secret that we live in an age-obsessed society. Like it or not, **"interviewing younger"** is the new catchphrase. Interviewing younger and being perceived as more youthful at the office is a vocabulary, a body language and a look. And here's a secret: These rules apply even more when your boss is your age or even older. If you are not willing to play the game, there is always somebody waiting in the wings who will.

Stephen's 5 Tips To Achieve A Younger Persona:

Rule #1: If you are over 40, be on Facebook. If you don't know how to join, let your kids show you, or even better, have a young person at work "reverse mentor" you on how it works. Let that same person help you choose your profile.

Rule #2: Do not disclose your SAT scores. If for some ungodly reason you still remember your SAT scores, keep them to yourself. Not only does no one care, but the scoring isn't even the same anymore, and you'll just wind up aging yourself.

Rule #3: Skip the cologne and excessive perfume. And while we're on the subject, wear deodorant. You may laugh, but many people just don't do it.

Rule #4: Practice "sounding younger" on the phone. Take a small survey of how old you sound on the phone, and then *practice with a friend sounding younger. (A tip: Talk higher and peppier.)* This is critical. In the same vein, make sure your outgoing voicemail message isn't too long or boring. Short and sweet with a positive attitude is all you need.

Rule #5: Dress age-appropriate. Never be frumpy. Always be classy - not trashy.

Two More Things

First, many women today are going back to work as executive interns. They are doing it to get reacquainted with the changing workplace and also to learn new and necessary skills for re-entering the world of business.

Before I started my new business I interned at WNYC the public radio station in New York City. Was it challenging? You bet! Working for a stipend and having your bosses young enough to be your kids takes some getting used to, but the communication skills I learned there I am still using today. *Many companies are offering executive intern programs especially the ones who do their business online.* Check out this newest way of brushing up – it's cheaper than going back to school.

Second, is a reminder from the "I CREATE" model. Whether you are in business for yourself or working for somebody else it's always a good idea to find a coach to help you navigate the waters. The key is knowing who is the best possible person to work with.

This is how I choose a coach.

I will only work with someone who is already successfully doing what I ultimately want to do. That means someone who walks the talk, not someone who just talks a good game. Find someone who has found a winning strategy that works for them and that will work for you too. I don't think you ever are too big or too smart to have someone who is invested in your success. It's a team effort.

Chapter Eleven
Show Me The Money!

Creating financial independence is a very important part of the Real Cougar. It gives you a feeling of power, freedom and accomplishment. Having my own money was something I gave a lot of thought to even as a child. While other kids were busy spending their allowance I was busy tucking mine away in a savings account my Dad helped me open. I never believed money could buy you happiness, but even way back then, I knew it could make your life a whole lot easier.

I never wanted to rely on somebody else to support me, so it was necessary to find a way to make enough money to take care of myself. That's why I chose to work on Wall Street. Starting out I knew I could make more money in finance than on Madison Avenue. Of course, I had no way of knowing where that choice would eventually lead me, I just put myself in an environment where greater opportunities were possible.

As it turned out I chose wisely. My career evolved over the years. With a combination of luck and a lot of hard work I developed a true passion for trading. The real money came when I got very good at what I had become passionate about doing. *The money followed the passion, not the other way around.*

Every Real Cougar knows when she doesn't have to struggle to pay her bills it gives her the breathing room to focus on the what's possible, not the "what is". You need a positive mindset to accomplish your financial goals, but you need a concrete plan too. That's why I asked my friend Carla Douglin to help me create a workable strategy that will assist you in successfully getting through the process of accumulating wealth. Together we have 30 years of financial experience and we will give you what you need to start getting your financial house in order, once and for all.

What you are going to learn is the basics necessary for managing your money. It may seem simplistic but believe me, you need these preliminary tools. Without them you will be fighting fear and overwhelm, right from the beginning. Overwhelm is so all-encompassing that it doesn't leave any room for abundance you are looking for. You need to get organized for money to flow to you. *You need a strategy that works and this is it.* I can't wait for you to tell me how amazed you were when abundance started flowing into your life. That's exactly what is going to happen now that you are making it a top priority.

Every Real Cougar knows when she doesn't have to struggle to pay her bills it gives her the breathing room to focus on the what's possible, not the "what is".

You have gotten to know me throughout this book, and now I want you to get to know Carla as well. It's of vital importance to trust the people giving you advice on financial matters.

Before Carla shares her personal story with you, here's a brief introduction to this fabulous female.

Carla Douglin is a national financial advisor, foreclosure expert, radio host and author. She understands the financial burden many homeowners face when buying, keeping or selling a home.

Carla is the CEO of The Douglin Group, Inc., founder of www. foreclosurehelpdvd.com, and host of "Foreclosure Exposure Radio" (www.foreclosureexposureradio.com) on Voice America's Business channel. She authored The Foreclosure Workbook: The Homeowner's Guide to Understanding Foreclosure and Saving Your Home, and created The Foreclosure DVD – both available in multiple languages. She has helped countless people figure out how to regain their financial footing.

Carla's Story

All my life, I have had a hankering for two specific things: to run my own business, and to be financially independent. Being an employee never did sit well with me. Having someone tell me that I had to be someplace from 9:00 a.m. to 5:30 p.m. to do a job that could take me three to four hours, tops, really did not make sense to me. I longed to be an entrepreneur from a very young age. I remember reading personal finance, budget-

ing and business books in my late teens. In my early twenties, Multiple Streams of Income by Robert Allen and Own Your Own Corporation by Robert Kiyosaki sealed the deal for me. I knew that being an entrepreneur was the way to go. But what was my passion?

In my twenties, not only didn't I understand what my passion was, I didn't understand what it meant to be financially independent and responsible with my money. By the time I was twenty-eight, I was making $98,000 a year as a corporate trainer. Unfortunately, I spent my money like it was water. Clothes, going out with friends, vacations...nothing substantial (except for the memories), and nothing that built my bank account. I was a "dabbler" – dabbled in stocks, dabbled in real estate... I loved the books I was reading and craved the idea of organization and financial freedom, but with all that I knew, I put none of it into practice.

My passion eluded me until I was 30. I had quit my job and decided to make it on my own. I had no savings, no plan—only sheer desire (and with hindsight, a truly naïve idea about how to move forward). A couple of weeks after leaving steady employment, I went to a real estate investment conference and found out about foreclosure consulting – working with homeowners to understand the laws, procedures and timelines of the foreclosure process in Maryland. I gravitated towards it, and found that, with my training background, it fit me to a tee. I started working with homeowners directly and training investors on how to work within the confines of the law. My training sessions packed the house.

And then, I met him.

The man that I fell into a relationship with was a real estate investor who came to one of my training sessions. He was handsome, tall, well-spoken, devastatingly charming and had perfect teeth. He was "my type", and after asking me out the night we met, we quickly moved into an exclusive relationship. It did not take me long to fall in love with him, despite the fact that he had five children living with him and four children who did not. Normally, the selfish part of me would not have dated a man with one child, let alone nine, but I was in love. Shortly after we started dating, I put my business on "pause" to become a full time "wife and mother".

Now, I put "wife and mother" in quotations, because we never were legally married. I thank heaven for that every single day, because over the course of the three years that we were together, I completely lost my identity. It has taken great strides and serious work on my part to gain it back.

From the outside, we were the perfect couple - the investor and the foreclosure consultant. Behind closed doors, it was anything but perfect.

The man I was involved with was extremely controlling. He wanted to control every aspect of me – what I ate, what I wore, what friends I spoke to, how I exercised... the list went on. He recognized how smart I am, but always said, "I want to mold you into my perfect woman". He knew what he wanted, without having any idea – or even caring – about what I wanted.

The subject of money was no different. My money was our money. Whatever money came into the house was managed by him. He knew what was "best for the family", and because of his controlling nature, I didn't question it.

During the second year of our relationship, I came up with a business idea that steered me on the path that I am on today. This idea and the subsequent business that I formed around it – became my baby. It was as if the passion that I thought I had found with foreclosure consulting was renewed, but now, it was bigger, more alive, more encompassing, somehow. I fell in love with my business, and worked furiously on it for hours on end. It made me happier than I had been in years, and I was so excited about every little nuance.

As the business grew, I began getting more publicity, which made him angrier at me. He could not handle the fact that I was concentrating on something other than him, and he definitely could not stand the attention that I received from men, from women... from anyone.

The straw that broke the camel's back involved money. When an investor gave me my first influx of cash to expand the business, my life partner felt entitled to a cut. He said that he had earned it. As the British say, I was gobsmacked. I looked back over our history and saw nothing but nagging, fighting, con-

stant questioning, doubt, and a neediness that wanted to disrupt me from my path.

It was only then that I started to see my own issues – I began to see the abuse and what it had done to me. When I looked in the mirror, I didn't see the confident, beautiful, happy woman that was there in my twenties – I saw a scared, self-conscious, unsure person who had no control over her own life. That image shocked and angered me, but it was exactly what I needed to see in order to get me out of that situation.

It has not been easy... far from it, in fact. I am not even going to say that I packed up and left him at that moment, because I did not. It was months later when I packed one suitcase and left him for good. However, that was when the real work began. I had to ask myself how I was going to live my life differently, what I was going to be accountable for, how I was going to manage my finances and business so that I could not only survive, but thrive.

This is an ongoing process, ladies. I have not "arrived" anywhere other than at a sense of deep understanding and peace with myself. I still have money to manage, bad habits to break, a financial foundation to work on, and emotional cleansing to do, but just taking that ONE step – the step of realization that I was not the independent woman that I desired, but COULD be if I changed my circumstances – has taken me very far.

Everything I am encouraging you to do I have done. Every step was necessary—no shortcuts! Now that you have heard how

I got started on the road to financial independence, let's talk about how you can do it!

One last thing before we start. Let me say how honored I am to be a part of this groundbreaking book! What you have in your hands is truly a blueprint for change – an opportunity to re-examine, redefine, and truly relish the life that you live and the power you have as a Real Cougar. It is my sincere joy to assist in this process!

Money is a subject that creates a wide variety of reaction with women. There is so much hidden emotion attached to it, so many stories you have told yourself about not having enough or having too much, too much embarrassment because you haven't taken care of business sooner. You've heard that money is the root of all evil, but it's just not true. ***Money is just currency— no more, no less.*** You are the one that gives it so much power!

A Real Cougar knows that financial independence is a major building block in her foundation. It gives you a power and a confidence that is visible to others, but, most importantly, tangible to yourself. We are going to talk about how you handle your money, what you do with your money, how to protect and grow it and create security and peace of mind for the future. Think about it—if you had that sense of understanding about all aspects of your money, wouldn't you walk around with a spring in your step? Of course you would!

> *A Real Cougar knows that financial independence is a major building block in her foundation.*

This is a major step toward putting yourself first. You know there are too many women over 40 who have spent their lives taking care of others only to find themselves lacking in understanding of the important financial details of their own lives. You have heard the story time and time again: a middle-aged woman who experiences a major shock when her spouse dies or divorces her because she doesn't know how the money was handled. And that's putting it mildly – there are women who don't know where the checkbook is kept, how many accounts the family has and what financial institutions those accounts are held in, where the wills or life insurance policy papers are. They have always left those details to others. I have heard this so many times, ***"Oh, my husband handles all our money matters"*** ***and each time, I have to ask the woman, "so, what happens if*** ***something happens?"***

Are you letting the responsibility of your own finances slip through your fingers? ***Are you living beyond your means by*** ***spending more than you make or racking up multitudes of*** ***credit cards in order to keep up with society's pressures?*** I know it's not easy to resist – who doesn't want that new handbag or the newest pair of Jimmy Choo's? Who doesn't feel entitled to that spa weekend with the girls or that vacation in the Caribbean? These little indulgences can add up to a big habit of overspending if we aren't making a conscious effort to watch ourselves, and can *Do not get hung up on the past.* cause us to create massive amounts of debt. ***Debt is crippling,*** ***and the only way to stop it is by taking control of your per-*** ***sonal finances.***

Real Cougar Women cherish their financial independence. It's more than "bringing home the bacon and frying it up in the pan," it extends to tracking the dividends on your investments and being able to quickly put your hands on your home insurance policy in case the pan catches fire. It's about every detail of your life. It's about planning, caring for and growing your foundation.

Financial independence is a conscious, lifetime habit that must be actively embarked upon and fostered daily and there's no time like the present to get started! Do not get hung up on the past – if you have not had a great financial track record up to this point, don't sweat it. Start now. Make the decision now to get your finances in order and build a money blueprint that will create the stability and growth you truly want.

This is how you get started

Step One: The 4-Week Notebook Challenge.

It's time to take a clear, honest look at your current financial picture. The full picture, Cougars and that means facing up to the good, the bad, and the ugly. The best way to do this is without judgment for your past actions and with an attitude of change. Realize this – by taking this step, you are *embracing* change to the fullest! You are truly stepping up the plate and claiming your freedom. ***Realize real freedom only comes when you get real with yourself.*** By understanding exactly where you are in your financial journey, you can create a realistic, easy-to-navigate map to get you exactly where you want to go.

Start by doing this. It may take you a couple of weeks to complete, but, with diligent and thoughtful action, you'll see how easy it is to start creating a solid financial foundation.

1. Gather all your pay stubs, bank statements, investment records - all the papers that *show you the money*. If you do not have this information handy, it's easy to get. Most banks and investment firms have online capabilities that allow you to log into your accounts and download your records. For your pay stubs, your Human Resources Department will have copies that they are happy to provide.

2. Use these documents to calculate your current income, investments and liquid cash. How much do you make on a monthly and yearly basis after taxes? How much are you automatically investing in a 401(K) account or retirement vehicle such as an IRA (individual retirement account)? How much cash have you saved, and where is it being held?

3. Gather all your bills – mortgage or rent statements, utility bills, monthly credit card notices, etc. At this point, do not focus on whether these bills are up to date or not. The purpose of this exercise is to gather data.

4. Use this set of documents to calculate your current monthly expenses. How much are you spending on necessities and how much are you spending on extras on a monthly basis?

5. Once you have your income and expense documentation, create a budget on paper, or use a budget spreadsheet or financial software (such as Quicken or Microsoft Money). Using a spreadsheet or software for budgeting has the advantage of allowing you to easily adjust different expenses to easily see how your budget is affected, but you can do this on paper as well. This is just your first pass at your expense amounts – it does not have to be exact or specific at this point.

Now let's take this exercise a step further. To sit down with your paperwork may not take you any longer than one afternoon. However, I stated at the beginning that this may take you a couple of weeks to complete. Let me explain…

When it comes to financial tracking, just looking at your statements may not go far enough. Many of us spend countless dollars and cents daily and have no idea where the money goes! For example, how much do you spend on your two-a-day latte habit? Do you smoke? If so, how much does a pack of cigarettes cost, and how many do you buy in a week? How easy is it for you to grab $20 from the local ATM to buy lunch? How much do you spend on parking? All the "little things" add up to big money if you're not watching, so to be truly accurate with your expenses… here's a challenge for you – let's call it, *"The 4-Week Notebook Challenge."*

Invest in a small, spiral-bound notebook and keep it on your person at all times. In this notebook, you are going to record how much you spend *every time you open your wallet.* Yes, Cougars -all spending. Everything. If it is $1.57 for a bottle of water, seventy-five cents for the parking meter, $50 towards the monthly phone bill, or $435 for that great pair of leopard-print stilettos on Zappos.com, write it down. Also, write down your method of payment (credit card, debit card, PayPal, cash, etc.). Then write down why you spent the money. This will not only help you track your spending habits, but clearly help you see your spending triggers.

Do this, without judgment, for four weeks. At the end of the month, compare your initial expense numbers with the actual spending to see how they add up. You will then be able to accurately assess your expenses and look for areas to adjust.

This is a very important exercise. Most of us have started money-tracking activities at some time in our lives, but the pressures and distractions of our daily lives allow us to put our budgets on the backburner. *One of the greatest foundational habits you can cultivate is knowing where your money is, how you intend to spend it and how your savings plan is working.* Schedule 15 minutes each day to focus on your personal budget – you may find that some days you only need to spend 5 minutes while on other days 30 minutes but be ready to do whatever it takes.

If you are already tracking your spending, congratulations! You are a woman on top of her game! However, we can all use a "refresher course" every once in a while in order to perfect our technique, which is why the *4-Week Notebook Challenge* is a good thing to implement at any time.

Does this budget stuff all seem a bit overwhelming? Well, don't worry – Carla has created a sample budget for you to start with! You can download it for free at www.carladouglin.com/therealcougarwoman

The Importance of Separate Bank Accounts

As you are developing your budget and mapping out your financial plan, both Carla and I strongly advise creating and keeping a bank account separate from your spouse. Your money is your own – whether you earn it through working a job, profits/interest from investments, or receive an "allowance" from a working spouse – that is yours to manage, spend, and grow. Creating an account that is separate from your household account and/or from a joint account that you have with another fosters a sense of independence and confidence in your ability to manage your own funds. If you do not have a separate bank account, open one as soon as posssible.

Step Two: Getting rid of the clutter

By the way… what did you do with the papers you gathered for the budget exercise?

Organization of all of your financial information is key to money success. One of the biggest complaints that women have told me about their money matters is that they have no idea where everything is – checkbooks, statements, tax returns – and *clutter impedes progress*. So once you have taken the time to gather your information, you've got to create a system in which to keep it organized and easily accessible from this point forward.

Here's a simple system for keeping track. You will need the following:

1. A dedicated space in your home to work on your finances – keep it clean, organized and stocked with pens, pencils, a calculator, stamps, Post-It notes, envelopes, and a highlighter. This is also where you will keep your checkbook and register in a special box or drawer for easy access.

2. A five-tier organization rack that can be placed on your kitchen counter or desktop to hold file folders, incoming and outgoing mail.

3. Four tabbed file folders for the organization rack. Label these folders *Receipts, To Be Paid (Bills), To Be Filed, and Outgoing Mail.*

4. A filing drawer with hanging file folders.

5. A shredder – preferably a cross-cut, multi-page shredder with the ability to shred credit cards.

After gathering these items, the first thing to do is create a Financial Facts Organizer in your filing drawer. Your Financial Facts Organizer should be placed at the front of your filing drawer (preferably in colored folders so it is easily identifiable), and is divided into three sections:

1. General banking information, which includes a list of any and all banks and account numbers (with phone number and address information).

2. Online websites, registrations, and passwords. These are critical tools in financial planning. So much of what we do and how we organize our money is done on the Internet, but how often have you asked yourself, "Now, what was the password?" Make sure to keep all your passwords in a place where you can easily find them.

3. List of your regular monthly bills, including company name, account numbers and contact information. You will want to list all of your bills here, including mortgage, utilities, credit cards, and any other miscellaneous debt that needs to be paid.

You will also want to create a hanging file folder for each month of the year.

Here is how you put your newfound organization structure into action.

First, it all starts with mail sorting. As soon as you receive your mail, take it to your dedicated space and sort it into piles: bills, important financial/family papers, junk mail, correspondence, and miscellaneous items. Immediately shred your junk mail and any unwanted credit offers – this will cut the chances of identity theft.

Next, place the bills into the **To Be Paid (Bills)** folder located in the organization rack, and the important financial or family papers into the To Be Filed folder. These bills are stored here until payday or a specific day you have preset for bill paying and budget tracking. You must pick a specific day of the month to pay your bills and make sure you note that day in your electronic calendar or day planner.

On your bill pay day, access your bills from the **To Be Paid** folder. Whether you write checks for your bills or pay them online through your bank website, use this time to check all financial websites to check balances and regulate your budget. As you are paying all necessary bills, write the date paid and check number or online confirmation number on the bill stub. The bills that need to get mailed are put in the **Outgoing Mail** folder on the five-tier organizer, and any bills being paid online are checked to make sure they have gone through or are pending.

Next, you will file the bill stubs, receipts and any other financial papers received from the **To Be Filed** folder into your monthly hanging file folders. When placing your paperwork in the folders, you should store them in chronological order – it allows you to quickly look through your activities for the month and find information about what was paid and when. You can review each of your monthly file folders at the end of the year to permanently store what is needed and shred unwanted paperwork.

NOTE: You also want to ensure that you have folders for your other important paperwork – namely, your will, any and all insurance policies (including life, health, disability, and car insurance), mortgage documentation, warranties, and medical information. In fact, you should make a copy of all of this important documentation and keep the copies in a safe deposit box at your local bank.

Once you have set up this system, you must respect it! *A system only works if you work it.*

Step Three: Building Blocks for the Future

Earning the money is only half of the equation. The second half is knowing how to manage it wisely. Now that you have seen a snapshot of where your money is and how it is spent on a regular basis, it is time to start planning for the future. To do this, you first need to understand your wants and needs. This is an exciting adventure for many of you who have never before taken a close look at all your pos- *Earning the money is only* sibilities. Now that you have *half of the equation. The* chosen to be a Real Cougar you *second half is knowing how* are ready to be clear about how to *to manage it wisely.* achieve what you want. This is very empowering and you will find the answers starting to come more easily and naturally than ever before.

So… what's your dream? Do you want to be able to live in London six months out of the year? Do you want to be able to buy a house for your child when they marry? Do you want to go on a cruise around the world? Do you want to finally start that business you've been dreaming about? Is your goal a simple one of financial security for the rest of your days? *Once you have identified what you want, you can create the financial plan to make it happen!*

Your financial plan should be a map for your short and long term goals. Once you have decided that then you can choose the asset vehicle that will help your money grow. The difference between a short-term vehicle and a long-term vehicle boils down to how quickly you will be able to access your investment and how much risk you are willing to take.

You have many choices available to you, and I know it can be confusing. That is why *I would strongly suggest that you talk to a financial advisor that you trust*. Ask your friends, your boss, your family if there is someone they would recommend. When you sit down with that person, ask questions and be very specific about your investment goals. *Your lifestyle should dictate your investment objectives.*

The list below will give you an idea of some of your investment *Your financial plan should* choices, with the pros and cons of *be a map for your short* each. Take this list to your invest- *and long term goals.* ment advisor and get him or her to explain them all in greater detail. **Let them know from the get-go that you are a proactive smart investor and that this is going to be a team effort. That's really important.**

It comes down to this. *You have the final word when it comes to your money.* No other person, even a professional, should be the sole decision maker. You must be in charge. From October 2008 through February of 2009 the greatest minds in the world of finance failed to foresee the collapsing economy. This isn't meant to scare you – just to make you aware.

Okay, now it's time to present some of the choices you have.

If you have a short-term goal to fund, you may consider putting your money into one of these investments.

1. Money Market Account: A Money Market account is where you put money temporarily while waiting to make other investment decisions. No money market account should contain more than $250,000 because that's what FDIC insurance covers.

2. Certificates of Deposit (CDs): A CD is a vehicle issued by a bank for a specific period of time. You purchase a CD for between $500 and $100,000 for a specific rate of return. The best use of CD's is to vary the length of time (1 year through 10 years). This is referred to as "laddering" and will give you a constant return of income.

3. Treasury Bills (T-bills): A T-bill is a taxable bond issued by the US Treasury Department. You can buy a T-Bill starting at $1,000. They are issued at a discount and redeemed at full value after maturity for a varied period of time. So, if you bought a T-bill from your bank at a redemption rate of 5% for one year, you would pay $9,500 at the time of purchase, and redeem it one year later for $10,000. All treasury bills are sold and guaranteed by the government at fixed yields. For longer term goals, consider growing your money in these investments for two years or more:

1. Corporate Bonds: A bond is a debt security, or loan made by the issuer, which are typically sold in $1,000, $5,000, or $10,000 increments. There are many types of bonds available, and the interest paid, time to maturity (when you can cash in your bond) and the terms available depend on the issuer. Rule of thumb: The rate of return on corporate bonds is dependent upon the risk you are willing to take. The higher the risk the higher the yield. (AAA rated corporate bonds have the lowest yields – CCC rated bonds and non-rated bonds have the highest yields.)

2. Stocks: When you purchase a stock, you are purchasing an ownership (or share) of a publicly traded company with all of the risks involved. Shares are traded on major stock exchanges (such as the The New York Stock Exchange and Nasdaq). You have an opportunity to make money through dividends (company profits distributed to shareholders) and through appreciation of the stock. Not all common stock pay dividends but all preferred share do at varying yields. Most companies that pay dividends offer their shareholders a dividend reinvestment program called (a DRIP) at no expense to you. Over the long-term this can be very beneficial if you are invested in a quality company.

3. Mutual Funds: This is a professionally managed type of collective investment that pools the monies of many investors and invests in stocks bonds and short-term money market instruments. The mutual fund has a professional manager who administers the fund. The net asset value, or NAV, is the current market value of a fund's holdings, less the fund's liabilities, usually expressed as a per-share amount. For most funds, the NAV is determined daily, after the close of trading. The public offering price, or POP, is the NAV plus a sales charge.

4. IRA's & 401k's: What is the difference between a 401k and an IRA? 401ks are sponsored by your employer. IRAs are personal savings funds. The advantage of these types of funds is that you can put money away for your retirement pre-taxes. 401ks are generally considered to be better than IRAs because they are sponsored by your employer. Frequently your employer will match a certain percentage of what you put away. IRAs, on the other hand, are simply personal savings accounts. You can always start your own IRA, and you can always put money into your IRA account, in addition to your 401k account. Additionally, you can deposit much more to your 401k account than to your IRA account annually. The more you save translates to higher net earnings, which is an added benefit to the 401k plan.

This is just a quick overview of the options you have available to you. There are millions of books and tons of information on the Internet about investing and both Carla and I suggest you take advantage of them.

Remember before you invest, always consult with someone who you trust and who is willing to show you their performance record.

I will l be adding an online financial forum for all the women reading this book. I also plan to have financial tele-workshops that are designed to further educate, support and answer your questions. You are not alone, so take a deep breath and smile as you start to move toward your new life of financial prosperity.

Chapter Twelve
The Law of Attraction
Times 1,000

The world as we have experienced it up to now is changing very rapidly. Climate changes, economic changes, the internet, healthcare - and that's just the tip of the iceberg. The energy on this planet is getting ramped up and all of us in some way are feeling the effects of this acceleration. Many are scared because they feel they are losing control, but now that you are a Real Cougar you are well equipped to handle anything. Change is opportunity knocking!

Here's another benefit of this heightened energy: What you want can be delivered in a much more timely fashion. It's a new paradigm. Compare the old energy to snail mail, while this new energy is email. What you have to do is learn how to plug yourself into this new higher frequency.

Change is opportunity knocking!

This will help you picture what I am talking about—you wouldn't tune your radio dial to 108.6 if you wanted to hear what was playing on 101.1. If you want to hear rock 'n roll you have to go to a rock 'n roll station. It's the same principle when you tune into universal energy. If you want a specific result but your dial is set on the wrong frequency there is no way you are going to get it. Figure out what you want and then set the dial in the right place to receive it.

It's the Law of Attraction times 1,000. Feeling good carries a very high energy vibration. Feeling bad carries a very low energy vibration. Emotions like sadness, jealousy, anger and fear keep you far away from the thing you want the most. Joy, appreciation, generosity and love open the door and invite it in. It's really that simple.

It always comes down to this—what do you believe? The glue that holds my world together, that makes me excited about getting out of bed in the morning, that energizes my business and my relationships, is my strong set of spiritual beliefs. Even though I cannot see, hear, or feel this connectivity, like many people say they can, it doesn't make it any the less real for me. All I know is the more time I spend with my dial tuned in to the higher frequency the happier I am. That's because I make my decisions from a place of knowing which means my intuition is coming through loud and clear. And, in the deepest part of my heart and soul I believe I am not working alone. It's my strong beliefs that have kept me sane though some really insane times in my life.

It's the Law of Attraction times 1,000.

In my humble opinion, there is just one elusive butterfly that everyone on the planet is searching for and that is happiness.

Too often we delude ourselves into thinking happiness can be found in external things like a new car, a dream house, millions in the bank or the perfect lover, but it can't. These things are merely diversions that deliver a watered down experience of what happiness really is. In essence they are all temporary band aids. There is one way to catch the butterfly and that is to rip off those band aids and *learn to love ourselves and love the things we already have.* When we are able to do that our dial is tuned into the right frequency. It's so simple, yet so difficult for most people. That is why Texas Tech University psychologist Jeff Larsen decided to put this "wanting what you have theory" to the test.

Larsen says, "Simply having a bunch of things is not the key to happiness." The results of his research show that you also need to *appreciate* the things you have, and to keep your desire for things you don't have in check.

In my opinion, Larsen is putting an academic spin on an ancient spiritual law that teaches us this: To get what you want, live as if it has already arrived. *That sets your dial in a place to receive.*

To get what you want, live as if it has already arrived. To illustrate how this works, I have included a story of another fabulous woman. Her journey has been a long one, but it has been nothing short of sensational.

Jacqueline's Story

By the age of 38, I was the model of the woman who had every-thing: four beautiful children, a long term marriage, a multi-million dollar business, prominence as a leader in my community and in my church. Here I was the picture of beauty, intelligence and perfect health, with nothing but years of success under my belt. True to my Texas upbringing, I thought I was invincible. After all I had mastered the "good life" modeled by my family and applauded by society.

Then one night in January 1987, my "perfect" life was dis-mantled when I crumpled on my kitchen floor in full view of my family. This was a total lapse in consciousness that came from out of the blue. I had no previous symptoms or warning to indicate that there was anything wrong.

After that incident, anytime I tried to resume my "superwoman" persona, I would experience the most severe anxiety attacks. Everyone around me was horrified, and so my life began to unravel. My husband was enraged that the superwoman support he was used to no longer existed. This disconnect eventually resulted in divorce. All the invitations I was accustomed to receiving, quickly evaporated. I was dropped like a hot potato by the social structure that had held me up. My buried fear of abandonment was glaring at me from all directions.

All the prayers in my heart, all the therapy I was receiving, all the inspirational talks in all the churches I went to could not relieve my pain. The devastating loss of everything I had spent my whole life achieving was just too much to bear. Unable to control my world or to conquer my grief with my normal indomitable will power, I was terrified and sought medical help. Much to my surprise, my doctor prescribed daily alone time to "look within" instead of prescribing the usual anti-depressant fix. As one who was addicted to perfection and controlling everything around me, I had no idea what "look within" meant and had never entertained the idea of "alone time".

Taking my doctor's advice, I began taking hikes into the hills behind my home. Over the next nine years, they became instrumental in my survival. Each day I brought my fear and pain to the forest and called to the Heavens and Mother Earth for Divine Intervention to heal and guide me. Without fail, each day my call was answered with what I now call "Divine Energy infusions". These infusions released my pain, and served as regenerative energy that filled me with hope, even though my life was still a huge struggle.

I did nothing to induce these magnificent infusions. The only thing that has changed was for the first time in my life, I was humble and open to receive help. This was a true contradiction of the "superwoman" persona that was identified with doing everything myself. Each day I simply surrendered and when I did I received the grace that brought me into alignment with my Soul and the Universal Power of Heaven and Earth.

There was just one flaw with what I was doing. For some unexplained reason I was unable to maintain this alignment in the daily grind of my life. My magic lasted only the 45 minutes during my alone time. I wanted more so I asked for the ability to bring this energy into my life 24/7.

My call was answered through a series of very powerful mystical experiences that taught me how to maintain the alignment. It came in the form of a Divinely-inspired Sacred Tool that I now refer to as "Diamond Alignment". Now I have balance and harmony that helps create extraordinary wealth in my life... wealth I enjoy spiritually, mentally, emotionally, physically and materially.

Over the last 17 years, I have worked to develop Diamond Alignment into a Sacred Technology which now brings the same alignments I received to individuals across the world.

The greatest gift of Diamond Alignment is the power it activates in us. It's a Spiritual Alignment that works with our demanding, accelerated lives. It's a simple commitment that takes just six minutes each day.

Diamond Alignment has proven to be the answer to maintaining this Spiritual Alignment in the fire of my life. It is simple, profound and available to all.

Jacqueline invites you to learn more about living a Diamond-Aligned life at www.diamondalignment .com.

Here are my 5 Tips for Connecting to Your Spirit

1. Believe you are a human being on a spiritual expedition

2. Believe you consciously create your own reality

3. Believe that it is your God given right to be happy

4. Believe you will get what you ask for when you are aligned with it

5. Believe you don't have to work so hard – go with the flow

This last chapter of the book is my heart. When I am connected to my spirit I am happy, and when I am happy everything I am working on comes together and produces results way beyond my expectations. This is why I know for sure what I am doing now was meant to be. Now it's your turn to follow your bliss and find out firsthand all the fabulous benefits that it will yield.

EPILOGUE

I feel this journey I am on is one that is necessary to soothe the longings of my soul. My soul is a tough taskmaster and lets me know very quickly when I am headed in the wrong direction. As excited as I might have been about certain projects I have been drawn to since leaving Wall Street, they just never worked out. I took that as a sign I had veered off track. That's not the  case with what I am doing now. Sure, like any business it has its ups and downs – but it's working. I love how it's growing and taking me in directions I never imagined it would. The best part is I am attracting so many wonderful people into my life and I feel blessed. This is just the beginning of our journey together and I can't wait to see where it takes us next.

Hello again!

I hope you enjoyed the book and are now ready to unleash the Real Cougar inside of you!

Do you have questions about anything you have read in the book?

If so, now is a great time to become a member of the Real Cougar community. When you join you will have a place to go that offers many different opportunities to continue the dialogue with me and many other members.

And here's how to get started:

First, I invite you to visit my blog; an up-to-date, quick read where I offer valuable tips and information. And here's where to find it: www.therealcougarwoman.com.

Once you get to my blog, you can also sign-up to become a member of www.therealcougarwomanclub.com. This is my elite online membership community that is for women only. It's great place to let your hair down and bond with other Real Cougars.

Of course, once you are admitted into the club you can also join the special group just for readers of this book. This is where you will be able to ask questions and voice your opinions.

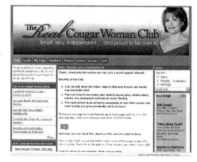

And I am also offering you a 10% discount on my new online teleworkshop - "My Next 40 Years" - Secrets For Mastering Life's Second Act. To learn more and to pre-register just go to www.dontevercallmemaam.com/discount.

I can't wait to meet you and welcome you personally into my Real Cougar Woman Community.

Warmest regards,

Linda

TreeNeutral

Advantage Media Group is proud to be a part of the Tree Neutral™ program. Tree Neutral offsets the number of trees consumed in the production and printing of this book by taking proactive steps such as planting trees in direct proportion to the number of trees used to print books. To learn more about Tree Neutral, please visit **www.treeneutral. com**. To learn more about Advantage Media Group's commitment to being a responsible steward of the environment, please visit **www.advantagefamily.com/green**

LaVergne, TN USA
18 November 2009
164578LV00007B/157/P